How to Remember Everything

D1534617

English
Math
Science
Social Studies

MEMORY SHORTCUTS TO HELP YOU STUDY SMARTER

Grades 9–12

by Russell Kahn, with
Tom Meltzer, et al.

Random House, Inc.
New York

www.randomhouse.com/princetonreview

The Princeton Review is one of the nation's leaders in test preparation and a pioneer in the world of education. The Princeton Review offers a broad range of products and services to measurably improve academic performance for millions of students every year.

The Princeton Review is not affiliated with Princeton University or Educational Testing Service.

The Princeton Review, Inc.
160 Varick Street, 11th Floor
New York, NY 10013
E-mail: textbook@review.com

Published in the United States by Random House, Inc., New York

ISBN: 0-375-76563-8
ISBN: 978-0-375-76563-6

Manufactured in the United States of America

9 8 7 6 5 4 3 2 1

First Edition

CREDITS

Series Editor: Russell Kahn

Development Editor: Sherine Gilmour

Production Editor: Evangelos Vasilakis

Art Director: Neil McMahon

Design Director: Tina McMaster

Designer/Illustrator: Doug McGredy

Production Manager: Greta Blau

Production Coordinator: Elfranko Wessels

Illustrators: Scott Harris, Thomas Racine

ACKNOWLEDGMENTS

This book would not have been possible without the contributions from a bevy of clever writers and the incredibly creative and talented team of artists and developers at The Princeton Review.

Love and thanks to Judy Kahn, my Mom, for inspiring the concept behind this series; she showed that an effective mnemonic never loses its potency.

Many thanks to Tom Meltzer, Jesse Jarnow, James Lakatos, Sandy Allen, Florence Lemoine, Eric Wolff, Scott Lieberman, Orf, and D. Marcus Arm for stretching their brains to add to the list of mnemonics.

I owe a great deal of gratitude to my cohorts in content, Ellen Gibson and Sherine Gilmour; thanks for loving the idea for the book series as much as I do.

To Tina McMaster, Neil McMahon, and Doug McGredy, thanks so much for putting in the extra effort and always wanting what was best for each page. You three are the real McCoy.

Much appreciation to Elfranko Wessels, Evangelos Vasilakis, Kim Craskey, and Greta Blau for their work on the complicated production aspect of this book.

Thanks to Barbara Heinssen and Tom Russell for standing behind this project from the get-go. The confidence was contagious.

Finally, our gratitude goes out to the one-and-only U.S. Grandmaster of Memory, Scott Hagwood. Thanks for sharing your wisdom and insight with our team, and good luck with your continued quest to share your memory techniques across the country.

CONTENTS

Your Brain and This Book: A User's Guide

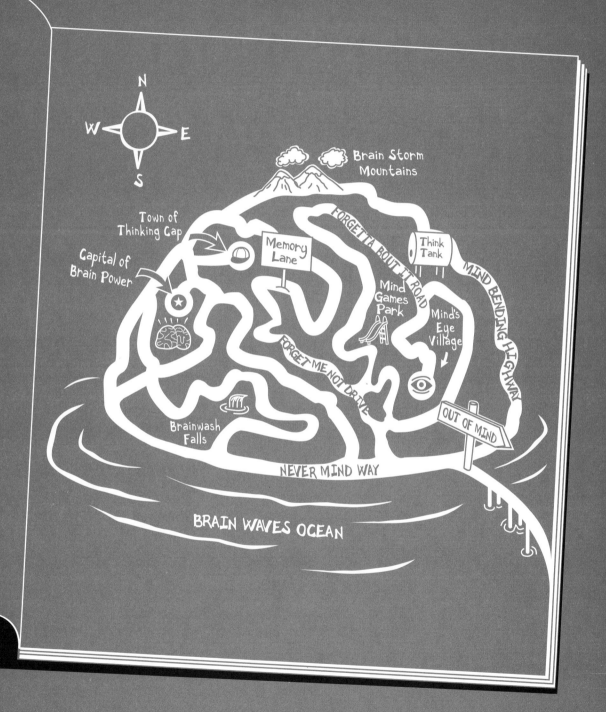

What Is a Mnemonic?

Hmm, *mnemonic* . . . isn't that the weird type of fish your grandma serves the family for Sunday dinners? Or wait, does it have something to do with astronauts and the space shuttle? It's got to be a kind of sickness, like pneumonia, or a kind of candy, like nougat. No, I'm sure it's that chemical the park used to clean the algae out of the pool last summer.

Hmm. Or not.

A mnemonic is a memory device. It's something that you can use to remember information. It's an effective and powerful tool that has been proven to help people remember details, lists, and all types of information. Mnemonics can help you remember *everything!*

There are even mnemonics to help you remember how to spell the word *mnemonic*. Read the sentence below.

▶ **M**ary **n**eeds **e**asy **m**ethods **o**f **n**oting **i**mportant **c**ontent.

The first letter of each word in the sentence spells the word *mnemonic*. Also, the sentence reminds us that using a mnemonic is an easy way to remember content. If you memorize the sentence about Mary, you can remember how to spell *mnemonic* and that mnemonics are simple methods of remembering important information.

Here are some other mnemonics for the word *mnemonic*.

▶ **M**om **n**eeds **e**ffective **m**ethods **o**r **n**othing **i**s **c**ertain!

▶ **M**y **n**anny **e**ats **m**y **o**range **n**apkins **i**n **C**alifornia.

▶ **M**onkeys **n**ever **e**ver **m**ilk **o**tters **n**apping **i**n **c**reameries.

The great part about mnemonics is that you get to make them up yourself. Sure, we provide hundreds of examples in this book, but some of the best mnemonics are the ones that mean something to *you*. For example, maybe you can remember how to spell *mnemonic* by thinking about evil monkeys:

▶ **Meeting nine evil monkeys on Neptune is creepy.**

Maybe you can visualize a gang of monkeys tiptoeing around napping otters. Or maybe it's easier to imagine a nanny eating orange napkins on the beaches of California. If one of those images sticks with you, you'll be able to better remember how to spell *mnemonic*. Just have fun with the image and let it bounce around in your brain. That's what makes it work!

Everyday Mnemonics

People use mnemonics to remember all sorts of things in their everyday lives.

Farmers use mnemonics to remember how to plant crops. Cooks use mnemonics to remember how to measure ingredients. Carpenters use mnemonics to remember how to use their tools. Doctors use mnemonics to diagnose diseases.

You've even used mnemonics to remember phone numbers, even if you didn't realize it. There are many ways to use mnemonics. There are also many mnemonics that can really save your hide!

▶ Leaves of three, let it be.

You can use this mnemonic when you're camping and need to use some "natural" toilet paper. You wouldn't want to mistakenly use poison ivy as toilet paper. So, this mnemonic can help you pick the best type of leaf to use.

Both the deadly eastern coral snake and the nonpoisonous scarlet king-snake live in the south and southeastern United States. You wouldn't want to mistake a deadly snake for a harmless snake. So, the mnemonic below may even save your life!

▶ Red next to yellow could kill a fellow!
Red next to black won't hurt Jack.

You can use the useful mnemonic below for lots of things: tightening screws, loosening bolts, opening and closing food jars. You wouldn't want to mistakenly tighten a screw that you were trying to loosen.

▶ Lefty loosey, righty tighty

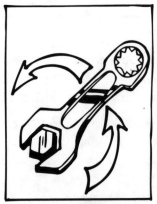

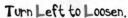

Mnemonics in This Book

There are many different types of mnemonics used by people around the world. We've picked eight of the most common and useful types to include in this book.

ACRONYM

An acronym is a word created using the first letter of each word of the important information.

We use acronyms every day. Here are some examples of commonly used acronyms.

4WD: **4-w**heel **d**rive

DNA: **D**eoxyribo**n**ucleic **A**cid

FAQ: **F**requently **A**sked **Q**uestions

KISS: **K**eep **I**t **S**imple, **S**tupid!

Laser: **L**ight **a**mplification by **s**timulation **e**mission of **r**adiation

NAACP: **N**ational **A**ssociation for the **A**dvancement of **C**olored **P**eople

NASCAR: **N**ational **A**ssociation for **S**tock **C**ar **A**uto **R**acing

NATO: **N**orth **A**tlantic **T**reaty **O**rganization

Radar: **Ra**dio **d**etection **a**nd **r**anging

RAM: **R**andom **A**ccess **M**emory

Scuba: **S**elf-**c**ontained **u**nderwater **b**reathing **a**pparatus

Zip (code): **Z**oning **i**mprovement **p**lan

You can also use acronyms to remember important information for school. Here is an example of an acronym you could use in school.

▶ PEMDAS

You can use this acronym to remember the **order of operations** when solving a math problem. You should always perform operations within parentheses first, then any exponents. Next, solve multiplication and division, from left to right. Finally, solve addition and subtraction from left to right. For more information about the order of operations, see page 150.

ACROSTIC

An acrostic is a sentence in which the first letter of each word connects with the intended-to-be-recalled information.

Acrostics can help you remember information as well as to conceal information. For example, if you wanted to write a letter to a friend and conceal a message, you might write the following note.

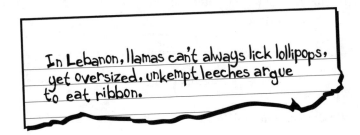

In Lebanon, llamas can't always lick lollipops, yet oversized, unkempt leeches argue to eat ribbon.

The first letter of each word spells a hidden message: *I'll call you later.* If your friend knew this code, then she would know to expect your call.

Here is one example of a commonly-used acrostic.

▶ **E**at **a**ll **d**ead **g**ophers **b**efore **E**aster.

This acrostic has been used by people learning to play the guitar as a way to remember the notes of each guitar string: E, A, D, G, B, E, in order from lowest to highest.

You can also use acrostics to remember important information for school. Here is an example of an acrostic you could use in school.

▶ **M**y **v**ery **e**nergetic **m**other **j**ust **s**erved **u**s **n**ine **p**izzas.

You can use this acrostic to remember the order of the planets: Mercury, Venus, Earth, Mars, Jupiter, Saturn, Uranus, Neptune, and Pluto. For more information about the order of the planets, see page 206. You may have heard of similar acrostics, such as **M**y **V**ery **E**ager **M**other **J**ust **S**erved **U**s **N**ine **P**ickles. It's okay if you've heard of a different mnemonic!

The best mnemonics are those that are easiest remember. So, whether it's easier for you to remember pizza or pickles, go for it! In fact, feel free to change any of the mnemonics you see in this book to make them more memorable for you.

CHAINING

Chaining is a way to link bits information by making associations between them. With chaining, you visualize a series of connected images or develop a story to connect terms.

You can use chaining to remember a list of chores to do, steps to follow in a project, people to call, items to buy at the grocery store, or other things. Here is an example of chaining.

Grocery List

I had a dream last night in which a lot of **eggs** made their home inside a **milk** carton. They built their beds with slices of **bread**. And their pillows were made with **cheese**. In the backyard of their little home, they had a creek flowing with **orange juice.**

Notice how this story describes strangely memorable images that include eggs, milk, bread, cheese, and orange juice. By recalling this unusual story, you could remember what to buy at the grocery store.

You can also use chaining to remember important information for school. Here is an example of a chaining mnemonic you could use in school.

► **What** thief could steal a **jewel** every **second**?

This simple chaining mnemonic can help you remember the definition of a **watt,** which is a unit of power. One watt is equal to **one joule per second.** If you can remember the hypothetical question about an overzealous thief, you'll know how to define the unit of measurement.

CHUNKING

Chunking is another way to link information using associations. With chunking, you group related information into smaller, more manageable categories.

Many people believe that humans can easily recall around seven different things or so at once. So, if you have a list of 20 facts to remember, you may be better able to remember them if you *chunk* the facts into seven groups (or less).

For example, we use chunking all the time to remember phone numbers. Most phone numbers (with area code) have 10 digits. This can be hard to remember, so we use parentheses and dashes to chunk a phone number into three parts: the area code, the first set of three digits (called the exchange), and the next set of four digits.

So, instead of trying to remember 3475559122, you would remember (347) 555-9122.

Try this out for fun! Say 10 numbers aloud to a friend, and ask your friend to repeat the numbers. Then, say 10 numbers aloud to your friend, but say the numbers as you would a phone number (pause after the third number and after the sixth number). Most likely, your friend will have an easier time correctly remembering the second set of 10 numbers. The same principle applies to your nine-digit social security number.

You can also use chunking to remember important information for school. Here is an example of chunking you could use in school.

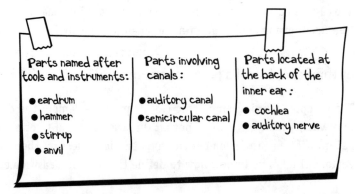

Parts named after tools and instruments:	Parts involving canals:	Parts located at the back of the inner ear:
● eardrum	● auditory canal	● cochlea
● hammer	● semicircular canal	● auditory nerve
● stirrup		
● anvil		

You can help yourself remember the eight main parts of the human ear by chunking the information into the three categories shown above.

KEYWORDS

A keyword is a familiar word that sounds like the word or information you need to remember. You've probably used keywords to help remember people's names. If not, you should try it! It's a great way to keep track of names.

How about if you met a boy named Frank? How could you make an association so that you wouldn't forget his name? You could imagine that everything he says is frank (meaning honest or sincere). Or perhaps you could form a mental image of him eating a *frank*furter—or even looking like one! Then, every time you see him, you can associate him with the image, which will help you remember his name!

▶ The name **Frank** sounds like **frankfurter**.

For example, let's say you meet a girl named Madeline. The first time you meet her, you can form a mental image of her going *mad*. Then, every time you see her, you can remember the image, which will help you remember her name!

▶ The name **Madeleine** begins with the word **mad**.

You can also use keywords to remember important information for school. Here is an example of keywords you could use in school.

▶ "A-gasped"

You can help yourself remember the meaning of the word **aghast** by using the key word **gasp.** If you can make the connection that someone who is aghast might gasp, it will help you remember the meaning of the word. For more information about aghast, see page 47.

The **Manifest Destiny** was the nineteenth-century belief that the United States of America was destined to take over all the land up to the Pacific Ocean.

The end of "manifest" sounds like "feast," which means to eat as much food as you can. So you can create a keyword mnemonic using this connection.

▶ "Mani-Feast Destiny"

. . . .
IT'S YOUR TURN

Remember, you can make up your own mnemonics or change anything about the mnemonics in this book. The goal is to help you remember the information, so include stuff that is memorable—your smelly pet dog, your teething baby sister, your favorite sport star, your least favorite chore, anything. Just try to make the mnemonic funny, make the mnemonic personal, and make the mnemonic make sense to you.

You can help yourself remember the meaning of the term Manifest Destiny by using the key word feast. For more information about **Manifest Destiny,** see page 101.

THE LOCI METHOD

The loci method is one of the oldest known mnemonic techniques. The word *loci* literally means *places,* and the loci method is an association of familiar places with information. For example, you might place certain information at certain spots in your room, house, neighborhood, or an imaginary place. Then, you can observe the details of each place or landmark as you follow a path, whether mentally or physically, remembering the information in the correct order.

You've probably used the loci method to find something that you've lost. Consider this example of the loci method.

Jordan had a great day with friends. But he lost his watch. He recalls the day's activities and decides to retrace all his steps to find the watch.

First, Jordan left home and walked to the park to meet friends. Then, they sat on the swings for a little while. Next, they went to a music store and looked at CDs. After that, they all went to the local ice cream place. Finally, Jordan walked home and checked the mail at the mail box before going inside. There was the watch! He had taken it off before getting home and put it down while getting the mail!

By retracing his steps during the day, Jordan was able to use the loci method to find his missing watch.

You can also use the Loci Method to remember important information for school. For example, you will be expected to know the four spheres of the Earth for your science class. The four spheres are listed below:

The **lithosphere** is the thin-but-solid shell of planet Earth. It includes the crust.

The **atmosphere** is the layer of gases surrounding the planet Earth.

The **hydrosphere** is the layer of water that covers the planet Earth, from the water in the clouds to the water at the bottom of the deepest sea.

The **biosphere** is the strip of the Earth where life takes place. That includes in air, on land, and under water.

► To remember which one is which, you can create index cards with those words and definitions and place them in the following places around your home:

The lithosphere card is placed **on the ground.**

The atmosphere card is attached to a string and is **hanging from the ceiling.**

The hydrosphere card is on **the sink, with the water running.**

The biosphere is tied to the **leaves of a houseplant.**

As you walk around your home and see the cards in their respective places, you can gain a stronger connection to remember each sphere. That will help you remember the four spheres of the Earth. For more information about the four spheres of the Earth, see page 209.

PEGWORD

A pegword is a short word that rhymes with a specific number and is easy to visualize. To use this type of mnemonic, you must learn the pegwords and the numbers with which they rhyme.

These are the pegwords we have used in this book. Notice how the number rhymes with its accompanying pegword.

A pegword mnemonic helps you remember things in the correct order. You simply choose an image to represent each thing you want to remember, and then tie that image together with the correct pegword. For example, to remember a first step, just imagine that step combined with a bun.

You can come up with your own pegword set. Pick a memorable thing that rhymes with each number. There are a lot of possibilities!

One	Two	Three	Four	Five
Orphan	Bamboo	Acne	Boar	Alive
Ribbon	Crew	Frisbee	Bookstore	Dive
Sun	Tissue	Zombie	Shore	Nosedive

Also, you can use pegwords to list more than five things. Just come up with words that rhyme with the numbers six, seven, eight, nine, and ten.

Six	Seven	Eight	Nine	Ten
Attics	Apron	Classmate	Clothesline	Den
Phoenix	Falcon	Crate	Porcupine	Firemen
Picnics	Lion	Skate	Swine	Pigpen

You can use a pegword mnemonic in your everyday life. For example, you might use pegwords to remember your class schedule because pegwords are helpful when you have to remember things in a specific order.

► Look at this example that shows you how a student could use pegwords to remember his or her first three classes: English, Math, and Science.

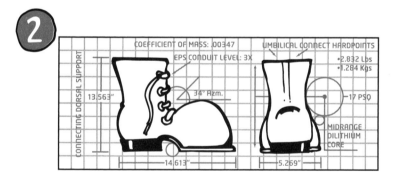

You can also use the pegword method to remember information for school. For example, you may study P. T. Barnum in your history class. Three of his major achievements from the 1800s, in chronological order, were opening the American Museum, touring with a famous opera singer known as the Swedish Songbird, and founding his Greatest Show on Earth, the circus.

▶ You can use the pegword method to remember P. T. Barnum's three major achievements, using the pegwords listed on the previous pages. See below.

The keyword for one is *bun*, so the bun displayed on the pedestal can help you remember that opening the American Museum was Barnum's first act.

The keyword for two is *shoe*, so the shoe with a songbird making its nest inside can help you remember that touring with the Swedish songbird was Barnum's second act.

The keyword for three is tree, so the tree with trapeze artists hanging from its branches can help you remember that starting the circus was Barnum's third act

For more information about P. T. Barnum, see page 106.

RHYMING MNEMONIC

A rhyming mnemonic is catchy verse that includes important information and rhymes. Rhyming is an incredibly helpful way to remember stuff. For example, the jingles in an advertisement often rhyme because the rhyme will stick in your head, helping you remember the product.

Even before people used written language, rhyming songs about historical events were used to pass on information. The rhyme helped the singers remember their songs and the historical information.

Here are some examples of everyday rhyming mnemonics.

▶ Thirty days have September, April, June, and November.
All the rest have thirty-one, except February, which has twenty-eight, and in leap year twenty-nine.

This mnemonic rhymes in the first sentence. In addition, it has rhythm. We use this to remember the number of days in each month of the year.

▶ Red sky at night: shepherd's delight.
Red sky in morning: shepherd's warning.

The words *night* and *delight* rhyme, and the words *morning* and *warning* rhyme, making the mnemonic memorable. This mnemonic tells us that a red sky at night may show that the weather will be pleasant, but a red sky in the morning may mean that there will be storms.

You can also use rhyming to remember important information for school. Here are examples of rhyming you could use in school.

▶ It's *i* before *e*, except after *c*,
or when it sounds like "ay"
as in *neighbor* or *weigh*.
(And *weird* is weird.)

You can use rhyming to remember spelling rules. For more information about spelling words with *i* and *e*, see page 52.

~~~~~~

▶ Seven spotted swans sat speaking in the sun,
using words with first letter repetition.
"What are these similar starting sounds?" asked one.
"My feathered friend, it's alliteration."

You can use rhyming to remember the meaning of the word *alliteration*.

~~~~~~

▶ You can add fractions that have the same bottom,
but only the top numbers sum.
You can multiply fractions any old time,
top times top and bottom times bottom.

See! You can even use rhyming to remember how to add and multiply fractions!

Figuring Out How You Learn Best

When we learn, we use our mind and our body. We use our body when we use our senses of sight, sound, taste, touch, and smell. We also use our body when we move. You can learn in many different ways. Everyone has strengths and weaknesses when learning.

Do you know how you like to learn?

Try to figure out what methods of learning work best for you. Think about a time when you've succeeded at school, at home, or with a hobby. Remember how you learned what you needed to succeed. Knowing how you learn best can help you make the most of your natural strengths and work on your weaknesses.

Imagine that your teacher told you to learn about the Andes Mountains. If you could learn any way you wanted, how would you want to learn?

KINESTHETICALLY

When you learn kinesthetically, you use your sense of touch or body movement. You may learn best by moving around or acting something out.

Would you want to learn using movement and your sense of touch? Would you get a plane ticket to the Andes Mountains, would you hike a nearby mountain, or would you pace your room as you studied what you were reading?

VISUALLY

When you learn visually, you use your sense of sight. You may learn best by looking at pictures, outlines, or maps. You may like to draw pictures to help you learn. You need to use your sense of sight to read and write too.

Would you want to learn using your sense of sight? Would you run to the library and read books about the Andes Mountains, draw a picture of the Andes Mountains, or go online to look at photographs of the mountains?

AUDITORILY

When you learn auditorily, you use your sense of sound. You may learn best by listening to your teacher speak, discussing with friends and classmates, and listening to music while you study. You may like to tap a rhythm with your pen or pencil while you study.

Would you want to learn using your sense of sound? Would you go on-line to download a lecture about the Andes Mountains or discuss the Andes Mountains with someone who knows about them?

Or would you use a combination of those methods? Using multiple methods of learning can often reinforce the information you're trying to retain, so don't be afraid to try learning in different ways.

Once you know how you like to learn, you can plan how you study. You can make sure you use learning methods that work for you when you study for important tests. You can also practice those learning methods that you don't prefer in order to strengthen your overall ability to learn.

Using the Learning Tips

Throughout the book, you'll find kinesthetic tips, audio tips, visual tips, "It's Your Turn" tips, and "Get This" tips. There are tips for each mnemonic. You can use the tips to help you learn and remember the information that's provided.

You can use what you know about how you like to learn with these tips. You may find that some tips match your learning strengths. You may also find that some tips ask you to work on your learning weaknesses. Don't hesitate to come up with your own tips, too, depending on the types of learning that you prefer.

Consider these examples of kinesthetic and visual tips.

KINESTHETIC TIP

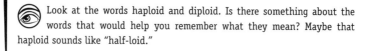 Read this "lefty loosey, righty tighty" mnemonic aloud and pretend you are turning a jar cap, a screw, or something else left to loosen it. Now, pretend you are turning something right to tighten it. Make faces to show how hard it is to loosen and tighten!

Each kinesthetic tip gives you a way to use your sense of touch or body movement to develop your memory of the information in the accompanying mnemonic. For example, acting out the action for the mnemonic may help you recall the subject matter.

VISUAL TIP

Look at the words haploid and diploid. Is there something about the words that would help you remember what they mean? Maybe that haploid sounds like "half-loid."

Each visual tip provides ways to use your sense of sight to develop your memory of the information in the accompanying mnemonic. For example, looking at images may strengthen your memory of the information.

AUDIO TIP

Read the complete "i before e except after c" mnemonic aloud and exaggerate the *e* sound and the *c* sound. Say it over and over to help you remember all the parts of the mnemonic.

Each audio tip guides you to use your sense of sound to develop your memory of the information in the accompanying mnemonic. For example, singing or clapping along to a mnemonic may cement the information in your brain.

Now, consider these examples of "It's Your Turn" and "Get This" tips.

"GET THIS" TIP

Each "Get This" tip provides you with fun, weird facts or anecdotes about the accompanying mnemonic or memory technique.

66 *Get This . . .*

Did you know that some people consider the sea surrounding Antarctica to be the world's fifth ocean? This body of water has long been differentiated by mariners as the Southern Ocean because of its distinct currents. In 2000, the International Hydrographic Organization officially recognized the Southern Ocean, although many organizations still disagree with this definition. **99**

"IT'S YOUR TURN" TIP

Each "It's Your Turn" tip guides you to get connected and involved with your memory and how you learn. An "It's Your Turn" tip may encourage you to come up with your own unique mnemonic to remember the content, or it may allow you to test your own memory.

IT'S YOUR TURN

Write your own sentence to help you remember the oceans in order by size— Pacific, Atlantic, Indian, Arctic. You can use the first letters (P, A, I, A) or parts of the words, as in the mnemonic above.

Memory Helpers

In 1940, the average 25-year-old adult in the United States had completed about eight years of schooling. In 2004, the average 25-year-old adult in the United States had completed about 13 years of schooling. That's a lot more information to hold in your brain! But don't fret—there's some very good news!

Once you have truly understood a piece of information, it gets stored in your brain—and it doesn't go anywhere. It is simply your job to know how to access it properly. Your brain is the greatest tool in the world; you just have to help it store and retrieve the information.

Here are some memory helpers that can help your brain understand, retain, and recall information better.

- **Be Interested.** When you are truly interested in the content, you learn better and remember information more easily. If you don't find something interesting, try to make it interesting. Try to think of ways to change the mnemonics in this book to make them more interesting—and more memorable

- **Be Critical.** You probably wouldn't eat a tuna-fish-and-tomato-soup ice cream sundae, would you? No, you'd probably only eat the tuna, or the tomato soup, or the ice cream sundae—but not all three together. You would be picky and choose one. Do the same with information you need to remember.

Pick the most important things to remember. You can do this by reading the titles and headings of sections of a book. You can skim sections too. Then, you can pick out what information is most essential to remember. Also, when studying, you can figure out what information you know and what information you need to know. Then, you can choose to study the information you need to know. You've probably done this before when you've highlighted a book, but the more attention you can give the most critical details, the better off you'll be.

- **Be Picky.** You can strengthen your memory of certain information by using your senses while you study. Try to involve your senses of sight, sound, taste, touch, and smell. Get moving when you study

too. Make sure to involve your senses in ways that will support your learning and your ability to remember. Read your books aloud. Imagine a mental picture of what you are reading, or draw a picture. You'll be surprised by how much your senses can help.

- **Use Your Senses.** Connect with what you are learning. You can do this by thinking deeply about what you're learning and by asking questions about the content. Consider how the information connects with your life, your experiences, what you already know. Make the information meaningful to you.

- **Make Connections.** Reviewing information often can help your memory. Try studying in short bursts so that you don't drain your energy. Review your notes before and after classes. And be sure to practice, practice, practice.

. . . .
IT'S YOUR TURN

As you read the mnemonics in this book, think about how you can make them more memorable. Mnemonics are only as good as you make them. No matter what, make sure the mnemonics are useful to you.

Ask yourself the following questions:
- Am I interested?
- Is this helping me to be picky about what I remember?
- Am I using my senses?
- Am I making connections?
- Have I reviewed and practiced?

Ready for a Challenge?

People around the world pit their memories against each other for prizes, glory, and the right to be dubbed the *"Grandmaster of Memory."*

ORGANIZATIONS

You can find out more about memory organizations by visiting these websites:

- Check out the World Memory Sports Council. Many countries are a part of the World Memory Sports Council, including the United Kingdom, Canada, China, Germany, Mexico, the United States of America, and others.
  www.worldmemorychampionship.com

- The United States of America is a member of the World Memory Sports Council. Visit the USA National Memory Championship's website for information about memory sports in the United States.
  www.usamemoriad.com

- The UK Memory sports council is a member of the World Memory Sports Council. Check out the UK Memory Sports Council for information about memory sports in the United Kingdom.
  www.memoryengland.com

COMPETITIONS

Memory competitions occur around the world. These competitions are like the Olympics for the mind, and they test the limits of human memory. People of all ages and nationalities compete with each other. Competitors are asked to memorize a series of numbers, a series of playing cards, a poem, random words, and other information.

Since 1991, the World Memory Sports Council has organized an annual World Memory Competition. The winner of this competition is dubbed the "Grandmaster of Memory."

Since 1998, the United States has also organized an annual competition called the U.S. Memory Championship. This competition is also called the U.S.A. Memoriad.

If you want to compete in the U.S.A. Memoriad, you have to be at least 12 years old. You can prepare and test yourself with the examples provided at www.usamemoriad.com/Archives/Archives.htm. You can find out more information by going to www.usamemoriad.com/Contact/Contact.htm.

Never misspell *misspell* again!

The Meaning of *Meander*

▶ When I meander,
watch **ME** w**ANDER**.

> *Meander* means "to wander aimlessly." All the letters in meander appear in the phrase *me wander*. Remember the definition of meander by remembering the sentence in the mnemonic above.

> Repeat the mnemonic aloud while wandering around your home aimlessly. Drift from one room to another without purpose and say "meander" repeatedly. Remember: Adding movements to a mnemonic makes it harder to forget.

The Meaning of *Abhor*

▶ **AB**solutely **HOR**rible

> *Abhor* means "to hate." It's a pretty strong word, so to say you abhor something means you must find it absolutely horrible.

> As you learn this mnemonic, tell somebody about something you *abhor*. Perhaps you find Brussels sprouts "absolutely horrible." Linking the mnemonic with something you really hate—out loud—will help you remember the meaning of *abhor*.

The Meaning of *Abridged*

The word ***abridged*** means "shortened."

▶ Check out the map below, and notice that a *bridge* makes the trip between San Francisco and Oakland much shorter. Without a bridge, the trip between two cities would take a long time. Travel on a bridge, though, and your trip will be *abridged*.

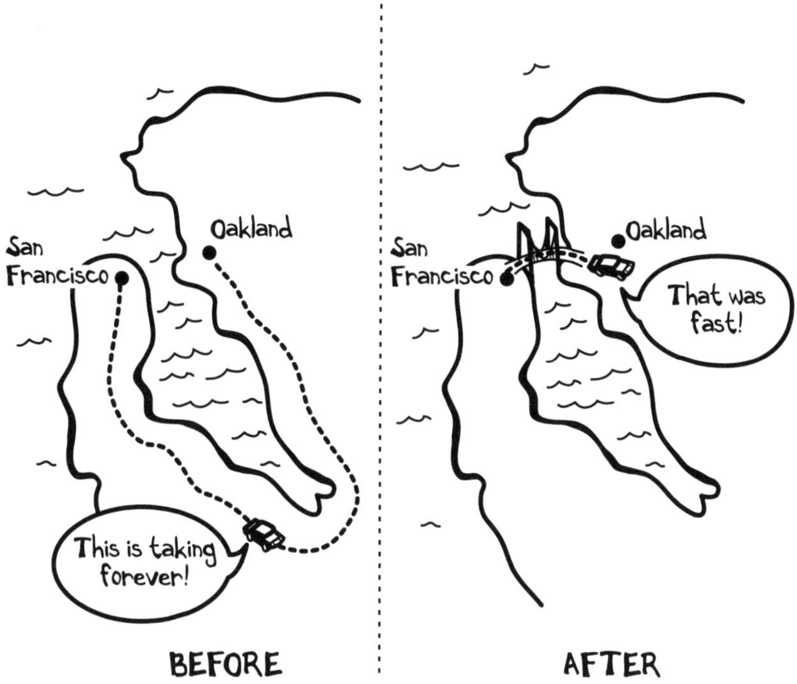

The word abridge is most often used to describe a book that has been shortened. An *abridged* dictionary is one that omits rarely used words. An *abridged* version of a novel is one that has been shortened to make it easier to read.

> **Get This . . .**
> The George Washington Bridge, the only bridge that connects Manhattan to New Jersey, abridged the travel time to get from New York to New Jersey when it opened for traffic in 1931. New Yorkers often refer to the bridge as the GWB—an abridged name for the George Washington Bridge!

The Meaning of *Impassive*

▶ **I'm passive!**

The word **impassive** means "emotionless." It also means "completely still; motionless." Remember its meaning by recognizing that the phrase *I'm passive* uses the same letters in the same order as *impassive*. When you're passive, you are completely still or motionless. You might also be in an emotionless state.

Get This...

The word *impassive* comes from Latin. It combines the prefix *im-* meaning "not" and *passivus*, which means "subject to emotion." Someone who is *impassive* is "not subject to emotion" because he or she is emotionless.

The Meaning of *Listless*

▶ Lisa made lists for absolutely everything: friends to call, groceries to buy, even things to do before going to bed (brush, wash face, lie down). It was her passion. She would get really excited about making and completing her lists, crossing off the items as she completed each one. But when she didn't have any lists, she lost all of her energy. She would be totally **listless**.

Listless means "lacking interest or energy." To remember this definition, consider the story of Lisa, who is interested only in making lists. When she has no list—when she is *list-less*—she becomes bored, tired, and uninterested in anything.

Repeat the word *listless* in a voice that indicates you lack interest or energy. You might want to sigh loudly before you say the word. Repeating the word *listless* in a listless manner could help you remember the meaning of the word.

The Meaning of *Aloof*

▶ **AL**one on the r**OOF**

The word *aloof* means "emotionally distant." Someone who is aloof prefers to be alone, away from the crowd.

Imagine someone who prefers to sit alone on a roof, and you'll have a pretty good mental picture of someone who is aloof.

Use the mnemonic to create your own rhyme, such as "Someone who's aloof / Sits alone on a roof." Repeat your poem while tapping your toe on the ground or thrumming your fingers on your desk. Adding movements to a mnemonic can strengthens your connection to the information, making it easier to remember.

The Meaning of *Cantankerous*

▶ Candice owned her own tank. She loved her tank, but her family was always leaving garbage in the tank, especially empty cans of food. The **cans** in the **tank** make Candice extremely upset, moody, and difficult—even quarrelsome. You could say that the cans in the tank make Candice **cantankerous**.

> The word ***cantankerous*** means "difficult, moody, and quarrelsome." Remember this meaning from the story that involves a *can*, a *tank*, and a *cantankerous* person.

 Draw a picture to illustrate the story. Drawing pictures can help you remember information.

The Meaning of *Ravenous*

▶ The starving **raven** ate **us**. He was **ravenous**.

> The word ***ravenous*** means "extremely hungry." It can also mean "excessively greedy." Remember these meanings by considering a hungry raven, greedily eating.

Repeat the word *ravenous* and its meaning, and then screech loudly like a raven. Yeah, it sounds silly, but it will definitely help you remember the meaning of the word! Even better, you can use the word in context too; next time you're about to have dinner, state "I am *ravenous*" before screeching loudly like a raven and gorging on the food.

The Meaning of *Sluggish* and *Slothful*

▶ The slug moved along **sluggishly**.

The word **sluggish** means "slow and lazy." To remember the definition of sluggish, think of a slug, a small, slow-moving, snaillike creature. They're one of the slowest creatures on the planet.

The same rule applies to the word **slothful**, a word that means "lazy." A sloth is an animal that spends only about 10 percent of its day actually moving, and it sleeps for as much as 15 hours a day. And when it moves, its top speed is roughly one mile per hour or about 10 feet per minute.

. . . .
It's Your Turn

Think of other adjectives that incorporate the names of animals (for example, bearish, catlike, dogmatic). Make up mnemonics that use the animals' characteristics to remind you of the meaning of the words.

The Meaning of *Ascertain*

▶ When you **ascertain**, you are **as certain** as you can be!

The word ***ascertain*** means "to determine with certainty." When you ascertain a fact, you are *as certain* as you can be that it is correct!

IT'S YOUR TURN

Look up the word *assure* in the dictionary. Make up a mnemonic for the word *assure* like the mnemonic for *ascertain* above.

The Meaning of *Misanthrope*

▶ I know a girl named **Miss Ann Thrope**.
The sight of people makes her mope.
She simply can't stand humankind.
I wonder if she's lost her mind.

The word ***misanthrope*** means "someone who hates humanity." This poem tells a story about a woman named Miss Ann Thrope that will help you define the word *misanthrope*.

IT'S YOUR TURN

Write a rhyming mnemonic for any of the following words. Their definitions are provided.

misadventure: an unfortunate event or result, an example of bad luck

misbegotten: received illegally

miscreant: a criminal or villain

misinterpret: to understand or explain inaccurately

misspend: to waste

The Meaning of *Revere*

The word **revere** means "to regard with great respect."

▶ You can remember the meaning of this word by thinking of Paul Revere, a hero of the American Revolution who is *revered* for his famous midnight ride.

Pay close attention to the illustration for this mnemonic. The depiction of Paul Revere performing his heroic task will remind you of the meaning of *revere*. So, too, will the depiction of the citizen watching Revere and expressing his awe for Revere's heroism.

Baron vs. Barren

Baron Ron and the Barren Tree

The words *baron* and *barren* are homonyms, which means that they sound the same but have different spellings and meanings.

A **baron** is someone who has great power or influence. In Europe, a baron might be a nobleman. In the United States, a baron could be a powerful business tycoon.

The word **barren,** on the other hand, means "producing little or no vegetation." A desert could be considered barren land because very few plants can grow in that climate.

▶ Baron has the name *Ron* in it. To remember that a baron is a person, picture a powerful man named Ron, like the guy with the crown, flexing his muscles in the picture.

Barren has the word *bare* in it. Land or plants without vegetation are bare. To remember this, imagine the barren apple tree with no apples growing on it.

The Meaning of *Torrid*

The word ***torrid*** means "extremely hot, or scorching." If the weather is *torrid*, you will probably be sweating and your face will be red.

► The color red is often associated with heat or warmth, so the keywords **"Too red!"** should help you remember the meaning of *torrid*.

Too red!

Picture a desert scene like the one above with a big red sun and a red-faced you. Insert any details you want which will help you remember "too red." For example, you might be holding a red hot poker or there might be a stream of red lava running through the sand. Really try to imagine what it would feel like to be there.

Not many people think that torrid weather would be enjoyable. In fact, most of us would think such conditions would be horrid. Since *torrid* and *horrid* sound alike, this could be another clue for remembering the definition. Torrid also rhymes with forehead (almost), so you can imagine being so hot that you have to wipe the sweat that is dripping from your forehead. Remember that you don't have to use our suggestion—choose a keyword with a sound that will remind *you* of *torrid*.

Staid vs. *Stayed*

▶ The **staid** person **stayed true** to his moral values.

The words *staid* and *stayed* are homophones. (That means that they sound alike but are spelled differently.) This mnemonic can help you remember the meaning of the word *staid*. Someone who is staid is calm and committed to a sense of what is right and proper. Staid people will always try to stay true to their idea of behaving properly.

Think of someone you know who could be described as *staid*. As you learn this mnemonic, picture that person in your mind. Associating the mnemonic with a person it describes will make the mnemonic easier to remember.

Denotation vs. *Connotation*

Many people confuse the terms *denotation* and *connotation*. The **denotation** of a word is its actual definition. The *connotation* of a word includes all the ideas associated with the word, but not the word's actual meaning. The **connotation** of a word is all the ideas that are suggested by that word.

The difference between *denotation* and *connotation* is indicated in their prefixes; use their prefixes to remember their meanings.

▶ **De**notation starts with the letters *de–*, as does the word **de**finition.

To better understand the difference between a denotation and a connotation, consider the words *ship* and *yacht*. Both words denote "a vessel for traveling on water." The word *yacht*, however, connotes wealth and conjures up images of a rich person aboard his or her own personal ship.

It's Your Turn

Make a list of at least five words that have positive connotations. Make a list of at least five words that have negative connotations.

The Meaning of *Bedlam*

▶ A woman comes home after a hard day of work. She wants to take a nap, so she goes to her bedroom. What does she find in her **bed**? A **lamb** taking a nap! Naturally she shouts, "That's crazy!"

The word **bedlam** means "a crazy place or situation." It can also mean "a state of extreme confusion." It is fair to say that coming home and finding your bed with a lamb in it would be a totally crazy situation— or bedlam!

"Get This...

The word *bedlam* was once used to describe a psychiatric hospital. Today, that meaning of the word has a very strong negative connotation (as do *nut house*, *loony bin*, and *funny farm*) and is used only by those who wish to speak critically about a particular hospital. **"**

The Meaning of *Cower*

The word **cower** means "to cringe in fear." The image above of a person cowering from a cow will help you remember its meaning—even if cows aren't very scary animals.

To help personalize the meaning of the word *cower*, create a mental image of someone you know who might be afraid of cows. (Or maybe it would just be funny to imagine him or her cowering in fear at the sight of a cow.)

The Meaning of *Rampant*

The word ***rampant*** means "widespread and out of control."

▶ To remember the meaning of rampant, imagine a *ramp* covered in *ants*. Imagine that there are so many ants on the ramp that the ramp is almost completely covered. Imagine that there are too many ants to control. That **ramp** full of **ant**s would be *rampant* with ants!

Repeat "ramp full of ants" and "rampant" aloud until you have associated the two in your mind. Saying the mnemonic will help reinforce it so that you will remember the meaning of the word *rampant*.

(You could also lean a piece of toast with jam against your home outside and see rampant ants on the ramp of toast yourself. But that would be pretty gross.)

The Meaning of *Alienate*

▶ You and your friends have a club. A space alien joined the club along with the rest of your friends. To celebrate your new member, you planned a big party with lots of delicious food. But before the party could take place, the **alien ate** all the food in your clubhouse. As a result, you kicked him out of the club and stopped being friends with him. He was **alienated**.

Alienate means "to be unfriendly to" or "to reject from a group." In the story, the *alien ate* all the food for the party—and was *alienated* from the club as a result.

IT'S YOUR TURN

Write your own story involving an alien who gets alienated! What did the alien do to deserve such treatment?

The Meaning of *Gruesome*

Gruesome means "causing horror, fright, or shock."

▶ It would be pretty gruesome if you **grew some** monsters in your ears, don't you think?

IT'S YOUR TURN

Gruesome and *grew some* are homophones; they are different words or phrases that sound the same. Make up your own mnemonic for another word using homophones.

The Meaning of *Imperil*

▶ A **chim**panzee was **pearl** diving when he got caught by an octopus. He was **imperiled**!

The *imp* in chimpanzee and the word *pearl* together sound like the word **imperil.** This mnemonic can help you remember that *imperil* means "to put in danger." In the picture above, the chimp has been put in danger while pearl-diving.

The Meaning of *Aghast*

► "A-gasped"

The word ***aghast*** means "struck with terror, amazement, or horror."

The illustration shows a shocked and frightened girl who is gasping. Because someone might gasp when she is feeling aghast, the keyword "a-gasped" will help you remember the meaning of *aghast*.

One good way to memorize a new vocabulary word is by acting it out or pronouncing it with the emotion it describes. For example, you could exclaim the word *aghast* as if you were truly horrified and hold your hands to your face or shield your eyes. If you do this a couple of times, your brain is more likely to remember the meaning of this word.

❝*Get This . . .*

The illustration above is a parody of a famous painting by Edvard Munch, called *The Scream*. In August 2004, this valuable painting was stolen from the Munch Museum in Norway. The two armed robbers simply pulled the painting off of the wall and ran out of the museum to their getaway car. Upon hearing this news, people around the world probably made the same face as the subject of the painting, *aghast* that something so terrible could happen to such an important treasure of the art world. ❞

The Meaning of *Idiom*

How to Remember Everything • Grades 9–12

When you hear an idiom, is it *music to your ears*? Does it *ring a bell*, or does it go *over your head*?

An idiom is an expression that cannot be understood from the literal definitions of the words. If your new jeans *cost an arm and a leg*, that does not mean you left the mall without two limbs. It means the jeans were expensive. And, if you ask your teacher how she knows you finished your homework during class and she says, *"A little bird told me,"* it doesn't mean that she communicates with pigeons. It means she does not want to tell you how she got the information.

▶ The picture on the opposing page shows literal interpretations of several idioms. Have you ever been *in a pickle*? That means you're in some sort of trouble, like the man in the pickle car who's about to drive into a tree! The expression *when pigs fly* means something is probably never going to happen. Picture this scene to remember the meaning of the word *idiom* and a few examples of idioms.

· · · · · · · · · · · · ·
IT'S YOUR TURN

Play a game called *Idiom Memory* with a friend or family member. You will need 20–30 index cards. On each index card, write one of the following idioms:

> break a leg
>
> face the music
>
> hold your horses
>
> know the ropes
>
> over the top
>
> rain cats and dogs
>
> rule of thumb
>
> skin of your teeth
>
> spitting image
>
> tongue in cheek

Write their literal meanings on a separate card. (Ask a friend or family member for the definitions, if necessary.) To create the rest of the word cards, come up with your own idiom pairs. Then, put all the cards in a pile, facedown, and shuffle them. Spread them across the table in even rows. The first player will turn over one card, then another card. If those two cards match the idiom with its definition, that player gets to pick up those cards. If not, it is the next player's turn to try to make a synonym pair. Keep going until all the cards have been picked up, and the player with the most cards wins. This game will test your memory and your language skills!

Here vs. Hear

▶ To tell whether to use **here** or **hear**, figure out for which one you'll need your **ear**!

Here means "at this place" and is the opposite of *there*, which means "at that place." *Here* and *there* are spelled with the same *–ere* ending.

Hear means "to listen" and is spelled using *–ear*. You need to use your ear if you want to hear!

Say the word *hear* out loud, and enunciate the *–ear* part of it. Touch your ear to make the connection that you hear with your ear—and that they're spelled the same way!

Emigrate vs. Immigrate

▶ When you **e**migrate, you **e**xit a country.
When you **i**mmigrate, you come **i**nto a country.

People confuse the words *emigrate* and *immigrate*. The letter *e* starts the words *emigrate* and *exit*; when you **emigrate**, you leave, or exit, a country. The letter *i* starts the words *immigrate* and *into*; when you **immigrate**, you come into a country.

Examples:

Enrique *emigrated from* Ecuador.
Ivan *immigrated to* Indonesia.

Repeat the mnemonic aloud, paying careful attention to how *emigrate* and *exit* begin with the same vowel and same vowel sound. Likewise, *immigrate* and *into* start with the same vowel and also the same vowel sound. Focusing on the similarity in the beginning vowel sounds of each word pair will help you remember the mnemonic.

Spelling *Repetition*

▶ To remember how to spell repetition, link the word *repetition* with the repetition of the letters *e, t,* and *i* in the word.

According to the book *The Elements of Style*, **repetition** is among the sixty most commonly misspelled words in the English language. Avoid this common error by remembering that the letters *e, t,* and *i* are each repeated in the word, and that each time the repeated letters are separated by exactly one other letter. The two *e*'s are separated by the letter *p*; the two *t*'s are separated by the letter *i*; and the two *i*'s are separated by the letter *t*.

Spelling *Attendance*

▶ To spell attendance, remember that you want to attend the dance.

Many people forget whether *attendance* ends in *–ance* or *–ence*. This mnemonic helps you remember that it ends in *–ance*, like the word *dance*.

Form a mental image of yourself showing up at a dance. Imagine that your teacher is there with a notebook taking attendance, making sure that everyone gets on the dance floor! Maybe he or she has a checklist to be sure that everyone does at least one mambo, one salsa, and two cha-chas. (It's not a terrific thought, but it'll help you remember how to spell *attendance*!)

I Before E

▶ **i** before **e** except after **c**
and when it says **"ay"**
as in **neighbor** or **weigh**

This rhyme reminds you how to spell words in which the letters *i* and *e* appear consecutively. In most cases, *i* comes first.

Examples:

believe, friend, thief

However, when the vowel sound is a *long a*, then *e* comes before *i*.

Examples:

freight, neighbor, weigh

Also, the word *weird* is one exception to this rule. Weird, huh?

Write a list of words in which *i* comes before *e* when the letters appear consecutively. Then, write a list of words in which *e* comes before *i* when the letters appear consecutively. Use words other than those listed in the examples above.

❝*Get This . . .*

Albert Einstein was one of the most brilliant scientists of the twentieth century. His theory of relativity ($E = MC^2$) revolutionized the perception of the universe, literally. But Albert clearly was no speller; Einstein breaks the rules of *i* before *e* in his last name not once, but twice! **❞**

Spelling *Necessary*

▶ You wear one **c**ap but two **s**hoes.

It's easy to misspell **necessary**. People misspell it *neccessary*, *necesary*, and *neccesary*. To remember that necessary has one *c* and two *s*'s, just remember that you only wear one cap but you wear two shoes. The *c* in *cap* reminds you that there's one *c* in necessary. The *s* in shoes reminds you that there are two *s*'s.

You can use the same mnemonic to remember how to spell the words *necessarily*, *necessitate*, and *necessity*.

Picture yourself on graduation day (finally!) getting ready to receive your high school diploma. Your advisor tells you that you need to wear shoes and a graduation cap to graduate. So that's all you wear, because that was all that was necessary!

Spelling *Academy* and *Academic*

▶ An acad**e**my is where you go to get an **e**ducation.

People who misspell the words *academy* and *academic* typically spell the words as *acadamy* and *acadamic*. They forget whether the vowel after the *d* is an *a* or an *e*.

You can remember that the vowel after the *d* is an *e* by recognizing that the word *education* begins with an *e*, and that an **academy** is a place where you can receive an education. The same rule holds true for the spelling of **academic**.

Write the words *academic* or *academy* on a piece of paper. Then, write, the word *education*, writing downward from the letter *e* (as if you were solving a crossword puzzle). You'll never forget the spelling of those words again.

Accept vs. *Except*

▶ Accept is an action.

People often confuse the words *accept* and *except*. **Accept** is an action meaning "to receive willingly." **Except** is a preposition meaning "all but." You can remember the difference by noticing that both *accept* and *action* start with the letter *a*.

Examples:

I'll *accept* an A+ for my analysis of American animation.
I enjoyed every example *except* Ethan's.

Say, shout, or sing the mnemonic aloud to remember it. Or, write a rap that begins with the sentence "Accept is an action." Try to come up with exceptions for items that start with the letter *e*. (Perhaps you like all animals except elephants?)

Stake vs. *Steak*

▶ A stake makes a tent stay stationary.
A steak is meat you can eat.

A **stake** is a piece of wood or metal driven into the ground. It starts with the letters *sta–*, as do the words *stay* and *stationary*; a stake is used to make tents stay in their place. A **steak** is a slice of meat suitable for broiling or grilling. Steak contains the letters *–ea*, which also appear in the words *meat* and *eat*.

The next time you eat a steak, act out a spelling mnemonic using other words with the "ea." For example, you could tell your mom that it'd be neat if she reheated it. If you're a vegetarian, tell your friends that nothing beats wheat—not even steak!

Affect vs. Effect

▶ Affect is an action too!

> **Affect** is an action meaning "to have an influence on." **Effect** is a noun meaning "the results of a change." To remember the difference between *affect* and *effect*, keep in mind that *affect is* an *action* (just like *accept*!).
>
> **Examples:**
>
> > Studying will positively *affect* your grades.
> > Improving grades is the desired *effect* of studying.

▶ You can also remember the difference between *affect* and *effect* with the acronym RAVEN:

Remember:
Affect
Verb,
Effect
Noun.

> As you recall the mnemonic, imagine the acronym above. Picturing the acronym with the letters **RAVEN** in bold print will help you remember its meaning.

Library and Librarian

▶ The **libr**arian is a **Libra**.

It's easy to misspell the words *library* and *librarian* as *libary* and *libarian*. Avoid this common mistake by associating the words *library* and *librarian* with the astrological sign Libra. The concept of a Libra librarian will help you always remember the proper spelling.

❝*Get This . . .*

The words *library* and *librarian* come from the Latin word *liber*, meaning *book*. Makes sense, huh? Spanish speakers will know the word for book as *el libro*. ❞

Complement vs. Compliment

▶ A **comple**ment **comple**tes something.
A compl**i**ment is something **I** always enjoy.

Many people confuse the words *complement* and *compliment*. This keyword mnemonic reminds you that a **complement** is "something that completes, or goes with, something." A **compliment** is "a form of praise." (After all, who doesn't enjoy a nice compliment?)

Examples:

The moving lyrics were the perfect *complement* to the beautiful melody.
I wrote the songwriter a letter to *compliment* his fine work.

Use the same mnemonic to remember the difference between *complementary* and *complimentary*.

Examples:

Yellow and purple are *complementary* colors.
Thank you for the *complimentary* comments.

❝*Get This . . .*

Mathematicians (and math students) use the term *complementary angles* to describe two angles whose measures add up to 90 degrees. Consider that the two angles complete a right angle, and you'll be spelling properly in your math class too. Angles don't say things to each other like "You're so a-cute" or "Your angle is adorable," so they're certainly not *complimentary*! See page 175 for more on complementary angles. ❞

Peek vs. Pique

Peek

Pique = quarrel intensely

Peek and *pique* are homophones that people often confuse. **Peek** is a verb meaning "to take a quick look at." The picture shows someone taking a quick peek. His eyes are two *e*'s to remind you of the meaning—and spelling—of *peek*.

Pique is a verb meaning "to make someone angry or excited." It is also a noun meaning "resentment." It has the letters *iqu*, which could remind you of the **i**ntense **qu**arrel that may result from being piqued.

All Together vs. Altogether

Which is correct, *all together* or *altogether*? And when should you use one or the other? To figure out these answers, consider a sentence that has either *altogether* or *all together*. Then, remember this simple mnemonic.

▶ If the meaning of the sentence changes when you drop the word "all," use **altogether**. If the meaning of the sentence remains basically the same when you drop "all," use **all together**.

Examples:

Let's sing the song *all together*.
That was an *altogether* enjoyable party!

Say a sentence with "all together" out loud. Make a point to pause briefly between the words "all" and "together" to stress that there is a space between the written words. Notice that without the "all," the sentence still has the same meaning!

All Ready vs. Already

The same rule applies to *all ready* and *already* that worked with *all together* and *altogether*.

▶ If the meaning of the sentence changes when you drop the word "all," use **already**. If the meaning of the sentence remains the same when you drop "all," use **all ready**.

Examples:

We are *all ready* to go to the game.
Did the game *already* start?

" Get This . . .

Sticklers for grammar insist that the word *alright* is always wrong; they say you should use *all right* in all situations. Some pretty famous and accomplished writers, including James Joyce and Langston Hughes, disagree; you can find the word *alright* in their novels and poems. For now, stick with *all right* if you want to avoid being corrected by any grammar sticklers you might know. **"**

–ible vs. *–able*

Is it acceptable or acceptible? Edable or edible? How do you remember which words end in *–ible* and which words end in *–able*?

Look at the root. If the root is all there (meaning it's a complete word), the ending is *–able*. If the root is incomplete (meaning it's not a complete word), the ending is *–ible*.

▶ –**i**ble = **i**ncomplete
  –**a**ble = **a**ll there!

Examples:

Roots that are all there
adapt + able = adaptable
agree + able = agreeable

Roots that are incomplete
poss + ible = possible
vis + ible = visible

There are exceptions to this rule, unfortunately. For example, when an "all there" root ends in *e*, you usually drop the *e*. The word *excite* becomes *excitable*, for instance. However, this isn't always the case. When the "all there" root ends in *ge*, you usually keep the *e* (as in *changeable* and *manageable*). English is a tricky language, huh?

Spelling *Calorie*

▶ A calor**ie** is something **I** eat.

Many people cannot remember whether calorie ends in *–ie* or *–y*. This mnemonic reminds you that **calorie** ends in the same letters that start the phrase "I eat."

 As you repeat this mnemonic, create a visual image of yourself eating a food you really love.

Spelling *Fluorescent*

▶ Under **fluorescent** lights, a miner got the **flu** from digging **ore** that had an unusually strong **scent**.

The word **fluorescent** contains the words *flu*, *ore*, and *scent*. You can remember this by recalling the story that incorporates all three words. Make up your own story if you prefer.

Repeat the mnemonic aloud, saying each of the three words—"flu," "ore," and "scent"—out loud. Mispronounce the word *fluorescent* as FLU-ORE-SCENT to remind yourself of the word's proper spelling.

Spelling *Forty*

The number **forty** is commonly misspelled as *fourty*. You can remember that the word is spelled *forty* and not *fourty* by imagining a military base with forty forts on it. That would be a very fort-y base, don't you think?

▶ A military base has **forty fort**s on it!

As you repeat this mnemonic, focus on how similar the words *forty* and *fort* sound. This will help you associate the two words, which will in turn help you remember the mnemonic.

Spelling *Government*

▶ We **govern men** through **government**.

The "nm" part of the word *government* tricks a lot of people. You can remember the correct spelling using the mnemonic above. While it's true that we also govern women, children, and pets through government, that wouldn't fit in the mnemonic.

The mnemonic "We govern men through government" has a natural rhythm to it. Set a beat to it, and add another line to the mnemonic to turn it into a rhyme. For example, you could add the following line: "We govern men through government / That's how my mnemonic went!"

Spelling *Separate*

Separate is a very commonly misspelled word; many people write it incorrectly as *seperate*. You can use the following mnemonic to always remember that there are two *a*'s in the spelling of *separate*.

▶ Imagine a man named Sep. His wife sees a rat in the house and calls to her husband, **"Sep, a rat!"** Then she screams **"E!"**

Act out your response to seeing a rat run across the floor. Jump on a chair, holler, or grab a broom. But be sure to scream for your friend Sep and say the mnemonic ("Sep, a rat! E!") along with your actions.

Spelling *Arithmetic*

▶ **A** **R**at **I**n **T**he **H**ouse **M**ay **E**at **T**he **I**ce **C**ream!

So now Sep's rat is hungry, and it's going after the ice cream! Just remember a mathematical rat is going to eat the ice cream, and you'll avoid making the common mistake of spelling **arithmetic** as *arithmatic*.

Write out the word *arithmetic* vertically on a piece of paper. Then, write this acrostic mnemonic on each letter of the word going down. The act of writing it out will help the spelling stick in your mind.

Spelling *Medallion*

You can think of the word **medallion** as the combination of two words: *medal* and *lion*. To remember this, link the proper spelling of the word to a story about a lion who receives a medal.

▶ Leo the Lion saved a town by protecting it from stampeding elephants. To show their appreciation, the townspeople gave a **medal** to the **lion**.

It's Your Turn

Make up your own story about a lion who receives a medal. Call him the Medal Lion to help remember the proper spelling of the word *medallion*.

Spelling *Argument*

Argument is one of the most commonly misspelled words in the English language. (*Misspell* is another, by the way!) By far, the most common misspelling is *arguement*. People assume the *e* from the word *argue* belongs in *arguement*.

▶ To remember that this isn't so, imagine two people arguing over a piece of gum. In other words, gum is at the **center** of their ar**gum**ent, just as the letters gum make up the center of the word argument: ar**GUM**ent.

The next time you see a friend chewing gum, demand that he or she give it to you. When your friend resists, start an argument over the gum. (You can explain later that it was all in the name of spelling; you can even show your friend this page as proof!)

Spelling *Committed*

People who misspell **committed** most often forget that the word has two *t*'s. They incorrectly spell the word *commited*.

To remember the proper spelling of *committed*, imagine that you have a friend named Ted. Imagine that Ted has gone crazy and needs to be committed to a psychiatric hospital. You have to take Ted to the hospital and instruct the doctors there to "Commit Ted!" The phrase *commit Ted* is spelled exactly the same way as is the word *committed*.

▶ Because he's gone crazy, you need to **Commit Ted**!

Do you know someone named Ted? If not, think of a famous Ted—Ted Turner, Ted Williams, Ted Roosevelt, anyone. Then, consider them wearing a straight jacket and bouncing around a padded room. They've been committed!

Spelling *Amateur*

▶ Your best friend is a captain in an amateur sailing race. You've offered to help as the First Mate. Midway through the amateur race, your friend falls off the boat—and you help him up. As you're pulling him up, he says "**A mate** you (**u**) are (**r**)!"

> Lots of people have difficulty spelling ***amateur***. You can avoid their troubles by memorizing the phrase "A mate you are!" The story above provides the proper spelling for amateur (a mate u r).

> Say the mnemonic aloud. Say it in your best fake British or Australian accent! (*Mate* is both British and Australian slang for *friend*.) Repeating the mnemonic—especially in a fake foreign accent—can help you remember the proper spelling of amateur.

Spelling *Embarrassed*
and *Embarrassment*

▶ When you spell embarrass, embarrassment or embarrassed, you'll be embarrassed if you don't double the letters!

> Don't suffer the embarrassment of misspelling embarrassment. Five of those letters—*a, e, m, r,* and *s*—appear exactly twice in the word. The other three letters (*b, n,* and *t*) rarely cause spellers trouble, so don't worry about them. Just remember that if you think there could be two of a certain letter in the word *embarrassment*, there probably are.

> Shout out the proper spelling of *embarrass* as if it were a cheer. Try it this way:

> E-M-B! A-R-R! A-S-S-!
> Embarrass!
> Embarrass!
> Yeaaaaaaaaaaaaaah embarrass!

> We recommend that you practice this cheer alone in your room. You wouldn't want to be embarrassed!

Spelling *Calendar*

▶ There are two *a*'s in c**a**lend**a**r: one for **A**pril, the other for **A**ugust.

Calendar is often misspelled *calender*, with two *e*'s rather than two *a*'s. You can remember that *calendar* has two *a*'s by recognizing that there are two months beginning with the letter *a* in the calendar. Those months are, of course, April and August.

While learning this mnemonic, purposely mispronounce the word *calendar* as cah-len-DERR, and then pronounce it properly as cah-len-DAHR. Stressing the *–ar* sound at the end of the word will help you remember the proper spelling.

Spelling *Lightning*

▶ Light**N**ing
Light, **Z**ing

The word **lightning**, meaning "a flash of light caused by an electrical discharge within the atmosphere," is often misspelled *lightening*.

To remember the proper spelling of *lightning*, use the poem above. You can change LIGHT, ZING to LIGHTNING simply by rotating the letter *Z* 90 degrees. Imagine that the letter *Z* has been struck by lightning, causing it to spin around until it becomes the letter *n*.

There is an actual word **lightening**, but it doesn't mean electrical flashes in the sky. *Lightening* means "the act of making lighter."

Examples:

The *lightning* hit the top of the tree, lighting it on fire.
She is *lightening* her hair by applying lemon juice.

Make a drawing to reinforce this mnemonic. You may draw the words LIGHT, ZING being struck by a bolt of lightning, causing the *Z* to change into an *N*. Or, you may write the words LIGHT, ZING and LIGHTNING with bolts of lightning for both the *z* and the first *n* in lightning.

Spelling *A Lot*

▶ **A lot** has **a lot** of little words.

A lot of people misspell this term. (Or is it that *alot* of people get it wrong?)

Consider the mnemonic above when trying to correctly spell *a lot*. When you use the expression *a lot*, you are using a lot of little words!

Another way to remember how to correctly spell *a lot* is to consider the spelling of *a little*. Would you spell it *a little* or *alittle*? If it's not *alittle*, then it's not *alot*.

 Look at the sentence "A lot of ants carry a lot of stuff to a lot of places." That's a lot of words, right?

Spelling *Independent*

▶ *Independent* starts with "I." But there is only one "I"—because the "I" is independent!

The word ***independent*** has a lot of vowels and can be a tricky word to spell. How many *i*'s does it have? How many *e*'s? Does it have any *a*'s? Just remember that independence is all about one "I." If you are *independent*, you don't rely on other people. So there's only one "I."

 Count how many *e*'s the word *independent* has. Can you make a mnemonic that reminds you to count the *e*'s? (Hint: Make it "*eeeasy*"!)

Principal vs. Principle

▶ A princi**pal** at a school is your **pal**, and a princi**ple** you believe or follow is a ru**le**.

The spellings of **principal** and **principle** are often mixed up. It's easy to understand why; they're pronounced almost identically. But just keep in mind that your *principal* is your *pal,* and you'll be set for the spelling.

Example:

My *principal* has *principles*: She won't let any of her students miss school.

 Go up to the principal at your school, and give him or her a hug and say "You're my pal!" Okay, you may not want to do the hug part.

Spelling *Shoulder*

▶ You **should** pat yourself on the **should**er.

Shoulder can be a tough word to spell. Note that *shoulder* contains the word *should.* If you remember that you *should* spell *shoulder* correctly, you probably will.

 Should you pat yourself on the *should*er? Absolutely. Do it!

Spelling *Cemetery*

▶ All the Es are buried in the c**e**m**e**t**e**ry!

Cemetery is one of the few words in the English dictionary that ends in *–ery*. The only other common ones are *monastery, millinery, confectionery. distillery*, and *stationery* (see page 75 for the spelling of that one).

To remember how to spell this unusually spelled word, consider the picture of the "E" cemetery above.

Spell the word *cemetery* out loud. Each time you get to a vowel, scream it! (You don't have to bother with the letter *Y*. It's not a real vowel anyway.)

Then vs. Than

▶ Q: When?
A: Then!

The simple rhyme above ensures that you'll never confuse *then* and *than*. Just remember that *then* answers the question *when*, with which it rhymes. The word **then** (with an *e*) identifies a point in time. The word **than** (with an *a*) makes a comparison.

Examples:

Q: When will you come to my house?
A: First, I will go to the store, *then* I will go to your house.
See you *then*!

Compare:

I'd rather read a book *than* watch television.
Enrique is taller *than* Kimberly.

Make several comparisons using the word *than* (of course!), comparing yourself to a family member, a friend, and a famous person. For example, "I am better than my brother," "I am hairier than Heather," or "I am a better shortstop than Derek Jeter."

Fewer vs. Less

▶ **fewer** sewers
less stress

This simple rhyme emphasizes the difference between *fewer* and *less*. Use ***fewer*** for things that can be counted. You can count the number of sewers on your street, for example. Use ***less*** for things that cannot be counted. You wouldn't say "I have 8 stress." You'd say, "I have some stress," or "I have no stress!"

Examples:

Meredith has *fewer* CDs than Marcus.
Russell has *fewer* pairs of shoes than Bethy.
Dina has *less* facial hair than Aaron.
Jordan has *less* interest in dogs than Jill.

Note: You can use the phrase *less than* with a plural unit that measures time, amount, or distance.

Examples:

It takes Chrissy *less than* 50 minutes to get ready.
Gabe has *less than* 20 dollars in his wallet.
Kyle drives *less than* 20 miles to work.

 Repeat the mnemonic rhyme aloud over and over and over until you know you won't forget it.

. . . .
IT'S YOUR TURN

The word *number* is used for things you can count; the word *amount* is used for things that you can't count. Make up your own mnemonic that will help you remember the difference between *number* and *amount*.

Which vs. That

▶ Bring me the **hat**
that is next to the cat.

I have an **itch**,
which is making me twitch.

Use the rhymes to remember when to use *that* and when to use *which*. The word ***that*** introduces a restrictive clause—something that is necessary to the meaning of the sentence. The word ***which*** introduces a nonrestrictive clause—something that adds information that is not necessary to the meaning of the sentence.

In the rhyme *Bring me the hat / that is next to the cat*, the information next to the cat is necessary. Without the phrase *next to the cat*, you would not know which hat to bring. The phrase *that is next to the cat* defines which hat is being described.

In the rhyme *I have an itch / which is making me twitch*, the information *making me twitch* adds information, but the information isn't necessary to the meaning of the sentence. Even without the phrase *which is making me twitch*, the sentence *I have an itch* makes perfect sense.

Examples:

Baseball *that* is played in the American League does not have a pitcher hit.

Baseball, *which* is America's pastime, is sometimes played with a designated hitter.

. . . .
IT'S YOUR TURN

Write three sentences that use the word *that* and three sentences that use the word *which*. Make sure you're using the words correctly by checking to see if the extra information is necessary.

Allude vs. Elude

Allude means "to refer to indirectly," as in "Marty didn't directly mention his friendship with the boss, but he certainly did *allude* to it often enough." **Elude** means "to escape" or "to evade," as in "Estaban *eluded* the dodgeball by ducking at the very last second."

To remember the difference between the two similar words, observe the reference in the mnemonic below.

▶ **E**lude, **e**scape, and **e**vade all start with the letter *e*.

Do you have a friend at school whose name starts with *E*? Perhaps you know an Eric, Ellen, Ernest, or Eugene. For one day, for the sake of learning the mnemonic, evade him or her in the hallways. Escape into a bathroom if you need to. Then, when you finally tell him or her why you were trying to elude him, make a casual, indirect reference to a friend whose name starts with *A*.

Altar vs. Alter

Altar is a noun meaning "a raised site used in religious rituals." People usually get married at an *altar*. **Alter** is a verb meaning "to change." (You could say that people get altered when they get married at the altar!)

▶ Notice that alt**er** is the v**er**b to avoid confusing the two words.

Alter a piece of paper. Draw on it, fold it in half, rip it to shreds; it doesn't matter. But when you're done, take note that alt**er** and pap**er** are spelled the same way—with *-er* at the end.

Stationary vs. Stationery

StationAry
Like an Anchor

StationEry
As in Envelope

The words *stationary* and *stationery* are very close in spelling. Only the *a* and *e* near the end of each differentiates the two words. How can you remember which has an *a* and which has an *e*?

The word ***stationary*** means "motionless." An anchor is motionless. Remember *anchor* to remember the meaning of *stationary* with an *a*. A boat with its anchor grounded will remain stationary.

The word ***stationery*** means "writing paper and envelopes." An envelope is part of a set of *stationery*. Remember *envelope* to remember the meaning of *stationery* with an *e*.

As you recall this mnemonic, imagine the illustration above in your mind. The pictures will help you link the *a* in *anchor* to *stationary* and the *e* in *envelope* to *stationery*.

Metaphor

▶ I **met a for**tune-teller. She said the world was my oyster.

A **metaphor** is a comparison between two objects without using the words *like* or *as*. For example, if you tell someone "You are a pig!" then you are using a metaphor. (Unless you are telling that to an actual pig, in which case he probably didn't understand you anyway.)

Say the fortune-teller mnemonic out loud, stressing the *met-a-phor* sound from "met a fortune..." Then, say "The world is my oyster," paying attention to the comparison being made.

Simile

▶ "I Like Your Sⁱmile."

A **simile** is a comparison between two objects using the words *like* or *as*. For example, "My love is like a red, red rose" is a metaphor because it uses the word "like." To help remember the difference between a simile and a metaphor, remember the mnemonic above. "Simile" is very close to "smile," and similes use the word *like*.

IT'S YOUR TURN

The next time you see a friend, say, "I like your smile." Then, try out a simile on him or her, such as "Your smile is like a window to your heart" or "Your smile is as bright as the florescent lights in the cafeteria." (Try to be nice.)

Qualities of an *Epic Poem*

▶ **E**xciting
Poem
Important
Characters

An **epic** is a long poem that describes the actions and adventures of an important person (or a group of important people). The characters are important for two reasons:

(1) They are heroic.
(2) They are typically among the greatest heroes of their civilization.

Examples of epics include *The Iliad*, *The Odyssey*, *The Aeneid*, *Beowulf*, and *Paradise Lost*. They are considered among the most important works in the history of world literature.

IT'S YOUR TURN

Use a dictionary to find the definitions of the terms *sonnet*, *limerick*, and *haiku*. Write your own mnemonic for one or more of these terms.

Gothic Literature

▶

Ghosts,

Omens,

Terror and

Horror,

In

Castles

A *gothic tale* is one that incorporates horror and the supernatural. Gothic literature was especially popular in the late eighteenth and early nineteenth centuries; that's one of the reasons why castles are such common locations for Gothic literature. (Another reason is that castles are really creepy!)

Classic Gothic works include *Frankenstein* by Mary Wollstonecraft Shelley and Edgar Allan Poe's short stories. Many modern writers, including Stephen King and Anne Rice, are influenced by the Gothic literature of the past.

As you memorize this mnemonic, draw a picture to illustrate each term: *ghosts, omens, terror, horror,* and *castles.* Drawing the pictures will help you remember the mnemonic.

Stream of Consciousness

Once I met this guy who had these lamb chop sideburns. He had an accent and may have been from Yugoslavia. That's a country that doesn't exist anymore. Anyway, this guy was wearing the strangest hat. I had never seen a hat like he was wearing and I could not take my eyes off of his hat, and he asked...

Stream of consciousness is a literary technique. Writers use stream of consciousness to represent the scattershot way in which the human mind works. Stream of consciousness writing often includes partial sentences, nonsense sentences, half-formed thoughts and ideas, and long passages lacking logic or focus.

Famous works of literature that use stream of consciousness narrative include William Faulkner's *As I Lay Dying*, James Joyce's *Ulysses*, Henry Roth's *Call It Sleep*, and Virginia Woolf's *To the Lighthouse*. T. S. Eliot employs stream of consciousness in his poem "The Love Song of J. Alfred Prufrock."

▶ To reinforce the concept of a stream of consciousness, imagine a girl talking in a stream of consciousness—with fish and boats coming out of the stream.

Write your own stream of consciousness. If you start writing about a stream and take it from there, then it may help you remember the name of the literary technique. Plus, it's *fun* to go on a tangent! (See page 188 to learn more about tangents.)

Foreshadowing

Foreshadowing is a literary technique that suggests what will happen next in a story. Foreshadowing provides hints of what is to come. In the illustration on the following page, four monsters stand menacingly. The four monsters cast four shadows, which foreshadows trouble for the person standing in the shadows.

One famous example of foreshadowing occurs at the beginning of the movie *The Wizard of Oz*. During the early scenes in Kansas, Dorothy talks with three farmhands and a mean old lady. Each of the characters set up their role later as they reappear in Oz as the Scarecrow, the Tin Man, and the Cowardly Lion; the mean old lady reappears in Oz as the Wicked Witch of the West.

Dorothy's encounters with the farmhands foreshadow her meetings with them in Oz. For example, the farmhand who later appears the Cowardly Lion advises Dorothy to be brave. The audience soon discovers, however, that this farmhand is frightened of hogs. The scene foreshadows the Cowardly Lion's behavior in Oz. Dorothy's neighbor wants to have the dog Toto "destroyed," and Dorothy calls her a "wicked old witch." This clearly foreshadows the witch's role in Oz.

It's Your Turn

Think of a movie or book you like that uses foreshadowing. Make a list of examples of foreshadowing in the work you chose.

FOUR SHADOWING

Stanzas

▶ "stands apart"

Many poems are divided into separate sections, based on a certain number of lines or a certain rhyme pattern. Each of these sections of several lines in a poem is called a **stanza.** Stanzas are sometimes referred to as verses.

The key phrase "stands apart" can help you remember that the separate sections of a poem are called stanzas. Each stanza in a poem stands apart—they are usually separated by spaces.

 Look at the following poem by William Blake. The poem has two stanzas. Notice how the stanzas stand apart.

The Sick Rose

O Rose, thou art sick!
The invisible worm
That flies in the night,
In the howling storm,

Has found out thy bed
Of crimson joy:
And his dark secret love
Does thy life destroy.

Onomatopoeia

Onomatopoeia is the use of words that imitate sounds, like *buzz* and *bang*.

▶ Look at the picture of a cereal box. The words on the cereal box— *pop, crackle, crunch, munch,* and *splash*—are examples of words that sound like the noises they describe.

Think of examples of onomatopoeia. Say the words aloud dramatically, making them sound the way the actual sounds do. Mimic the sharp "crack" of a baseball bat. Imitate the menacing "hiss" of a slithering snake. See if you can re-create the "pop" of a balloon bursting.

Genre

▶ **N**ever **p**lay **p**iano **b**eside **s**hort **r**eferees.

A **genre** is a type of literary work. Just like there are lots of different types of movies (horror, comedy, documentary), there are many types of literary works. The first letter in each word of the acrostic stands for one of the literary genres below.

- novel
- play
- poem
- biography
- short story
- reference book

Some of the words in the mnemonic also sound like the genres they represent. For example, the word *play* in the acrostic stands for the genre play, the word *short* stands for short stories, and the word *referees* stands for reference book. Keeping this image and the acrostic in mind should help you remember these genres.

In order for an acrostic to help you remember a set of information, you first have to remember the acrostic itself! One way to reinforce this acrostic is by pantomiming the act of playing piano beside short referees. To pantomime means "to express a story by moving your body."

Find a bench or a chair that you can pretend is a piano bench. Act out squeezing onto the bench between two other people. Then, pretend you are playing the piano with your arms squeezed to your sides. To get across the idea that you are beside *short* referees, you may look down at them irritably. Or, you could pretend to switch places with one of the referees. Then, you could hunch down to appear short and pretend to blow a whistle or gesture like you're calling a time-out. It may sound silly, but you'll never forget the sentence!

Exposition

▶ **EXP**lanation **O**f the **SIT**uat**ION**

Exposition is the part of a story that provides important background information that helps you understand who the characters are or why they are acting in a certain way. Exposition often occurs at the very beginning of a movie, play, or novel; it explains what has happened prior to the beginning of the story.

Example:

Character 1: Donnie has been awfully sad lately.
Character 2: Can you blame him? His mother died two weeks ago.

This bit of exposition helps the audience understand why Donnie is so sad. It explains the situation of the character. Exposition also helps to introduce the major themes of a story. Donnie's sadness is likely to be an important part of this story; otherwise, why would the writer bother to bring it to the audience's attention?

Chant the mnemonic above while stressing its bold letters that spell EXPOSITION. Repeating the mnemonic will help remind you of the meaning of the literary term.

Memoir

▶ **MEMO**ries **I**n w**R**iting

A **memoir** is a written account of one's personal experiences. Another word for memoir is *autobiography*.

 Start writing the word *memoir* on a piece of paper—but stop after the second letter. That's what a memoir is about!

Structuring an Essay

A well-structured essay typically contains an introductory paragraph, in which the topic of the essay is put forward; supporting paragraphs, in which details useful to understanding the topic are presented; and a concluding paragraph, in which the writer clearly states the point of the essay.

▶ Write the following terms on index cards:

introductory paragraph

supporting paragraph 1

supporting paragraph 2

supporting paragraph 3

concluding paragraph

Place the cards around your bedroom as follows:

introductory paragraph on the outside of your door

supporting paragraph 1, supporting paragraph 2, and **supporting paragraph 3** on the walls, in order as you walk around the room in a clockwise direction

concluding paragraph on the inside of your door

Enter your room and walk around it in a clockwise direction to remind yourself how to structure an essay. As you walk around, stop at each card and review the function of each part of a well-organized essay.

. . . .
It's Your Turn

Get a copy of your local newspaper. Turn to the editorial page. Read an editorial and identify the introductory paragraph, the supporting paragraphs, and the concluding paragraph.

The Five-Step Writing Method

There are five steps to creating a finished piece of writing.

Pre-write: Figure out what you want to write about. Brainstorm ideas. Think about your audience and how best to communicate your purpose to readers.

Draft: Write a rough version of your final piece.

Revise: Read for clarity and organization. Fix sections that are unclear. Cut parts that are unnecessary.

Edit: Read for spelling, punctuation, and grammar. Check word usage to determine whether you've used the best word for a particular situation.

Present: Share your work with others.

▶ Before you write a paper or report, take a walk to set up the five steps of writing.

Go someplace that starts with the letter *P*. Perhaps that's the porch or the pantry. Associate that location with the first step, *pre-write*.

Next, walk along to a place that starts with the letter *D*. Do you have a dryer? Go to it. Associate that spot with the second step, *draft*.

Continue along your route, forming location mnemonics for each of the five terms. Go to spots that mean something to you—the roof, Ed's room, and the printer in the den. You should be able to recall the five steps of writing a finished piece by traveling your route.

Draw a map of the route you used for your mnemonic. Mark each of the landmarks on the map, along with the writing step that follows the sequence.

Three Text Types

► There are three main types of texts. You can use your **PEN** to write them!

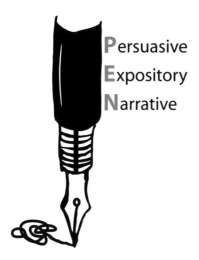

Persuasive
Expository
Narrative

The name of each type of text contains clues about its function.

Persuasive texts are intended to persuade: A persuasive text attempts to persuade readers of a particular point of view.

Expository texts are intended to expose: An expository text exposes the truth about a subject. Think also of an exposé, which is a journalistic piece that reveals secrets.

Narrative texts are intended to narrate: A narrative narrates a story.

It's Your Turn

Look through the newspaper or some of your favorite magazines. Find an example of each type of writing.

Gerund

▶ A gerund ends in –in**G**.

It's a v**ER**b

used as a no**UN**.

Don't you see?

The mnemonic poem can help you remember what a gerund is. It's a word that ends in *–ing*, but it's used as a noun (not a verb).

Examples:

Swimming is my favorite form of exercise.
I enjoy *cooking* Dominican food.
The *understanding* of a gerund is an important skill for English class.

Not all words ending in *–ing* are gerunds, of course. Some verbs end in *–ing*, and they are called *present participles*.

Examples:

I am *dancing* in a recital.
We are *hiking* up the mountain.

Dependent Clauses and Complex Sentences

▶ Because it starts with a **dependent clause**, this is a **complex sentence**.

The sentence above will help you to remember the terms *dependent clause* and *complex sentence*. The sentence begins with the dependent clause *"Because it starts with a dependent clause."* It is a **dependent clause** because it is not a sentence on its own; it needs the rest of the sentence to complete it.

A **complex sentence** is any sentence that includes a dependent clause. So, memorize this mnemonic, and you will not only know the definition of a complex sentence, but also have easy-to-remember examples of a dependent clause.

Sometimes you will see dependent clauses referred to as *subordinate clauses*. The two terms mean the same thing.

Examples:

Before Slade goes to work, he eats breakfast.
While Judy reads a book, she listens to the radio.

IT'S YOUR TURN

Using your own dependent clause, write your own complex sentence. In your sentence, you can use the most famous clause of them all—Santa Claus! (Perhaps he's dependent on Mrs. Claus for something....)

Common Comma Errors

Comma mistakes are very common. Some people put commas anywhere they hear a pause in the sentence. This can lead to commas where they're not supposed to be—and no comma where there should be one! There are a lot of comma rules, but there's one simple mnemonic that can help you avoid a lot of the most common errors.

▶ You need a comma in between two independent clauses that use one of the "FANBOYS" words.

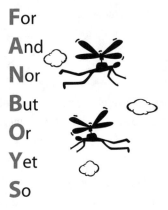

For
And
Nor
But
Or
Yet
So

Look at the following sentences. Each one contains two independent clauses.

Examples:

I do not need to practice basketball, *for* I am already the greatest player in the world.

I can sink every shot I shoot, *and* I can get to every rebound.

Michael Jordan wasn't better than me, *nor* could Magic Johnson take me on one-on-one.

I told my coach I'm the greatest player in the world, *but* he said he didn't think so.

He told me I have to practice, *or* I am not going to play on the team.

My coach is a talented instructor, *yet* he clearly doesn't know how good I am.

I want to play on the school team, *so* I guess I will have to practice.

Keep in mind that the FANBOYS words only include a comma with two *independent* clauses. That means you could take away the word and the comma and get two complete sentences.

Examples:

> I do not need to practice basketball. I am already the greatest player in the world.
>
> I can sink every shot I shoot. I can get to every rebound.

Sentences with dependent clauses would therefore not have a comma.

Examples:

> I can sink every shot I shoot and can get to every rebound.
>
> My coach is a talented instructor yet clearly doesn't know how good I am.

· · · · · · · · · · · · ·

It's Your Turn

Write your own sentence using one of the FANBOYS words with a comma. Be sure to include two independent clauses. (Can you take away the word and make two sentences?) To reinforce the "FANBOYS" acronym, see if you can get "fan" and "boys" into your model sentence.

Appositive

▶ An appositive helps you make **a positive** identification by adding information.

An **appositive** is a word or phrase that identifies the noun in a sentence or adds more information about the noun. An appositive is usually set apart from the rest of the sentence with commas. Three examples are shown below, with the appositives set in italics.

Examples:

Beth's cat, Jiboo, loves to walk on people's heads.

Tina, *a talented* actress, will be starring in the school play.

A grammatical term, *appositive*, is a word that means "a word or phrase set next to a noun in order to describe it."

· · · · · · · · · · · · ·
It's Your Turn

Write a sentence that defines the word *appositive* and includes the word *appositive*. Just remember that an appositive makes it easier to make *a positive* identification by providing useful information.

**Remember the Alamo—
and everything else!**

Major Causes of the Revolutionary War

There were three major British Parliament acts that led to the American Revolutionary War.

▶ The first major British Parliament act was the **Sugar Act of 1764**. The Sugar Act was intended to get money from the American colonies for the British government even though the colonists couldn't vote. The Sugar Act inspired the rebellious colonist slogan, "No taxation without representation." *One* rhymes with *bun*. To remember this first act, imagine pouring sugar onto a bun.

The second act was the **Stamp Act of 1765**. This taxed not only stamps but all printed materials like newspapers, legal documents, and even playing cards! *Two* rhymes with *shoe*. To remember this second act, imagine a shoe on a stamp.

The **Townshend Acts of 1767** were the third acts. The Townshend Acts put a tax on goods the colonists imported. As a result, the colonists boycotted British goods so that they wouldn't have to pay the tax. The British leaders responded by repealing the tax from everything except tea.

This resulted in the well-known **Boston Tea Party,** in which colonists dumped hundreds of chests of British tea into the Boston Harbor, ruining the tea and costing the British a lot of money. *Three* rhymes with *tree*. To remember this third act, imagine a tree pouring tea.

IT'S YOUR TURN

Close your eyes. Use the pictures to remember the names and order of the acts. Did you remember them correctly? If not, look at the pictures again. Pay attention to interesting details in the pictures, color them, draw them again in your notebook, or create your own.

Turning Points of the American Revolution

The War for American Independence was fought for seven years, but a few battles were especially pivotal.

▶ The **Battles of Lexington and Concord** in 1775 marked the official start of the Revolutionary War. It is unknown which side fired the first shot between the British redcoats and the minutemen and militiamen. But with advanced warning from Paul Revere, the colonists' militia earned a crucial early victory over the powerful British army. *One* rhymes with *bun*. To remember this first battle, imagine a bun on the nose of the Concord, which was a supersonic jet.

The **Battles of Saratoga in 1777** were a major turning point in the war for the colonists. The victory prevented the British from dividing the colonies in half by capturing New York State. But perhaps more important, it was the battle that persuaded the French to join the war on the American side. *Two* rhymes with *shoe*. To remember this second battle, imagine a woman named Sara, wearing a toga and standing in a giant shoe.

The Continental Army at **Valley Forge** suffered from cold, disease, and hunger throughout the winter of 1777–1778. But the soldiers endured, and their training turned the army into a disciplined fighting force. *Three* rhymes with *tree*. To remember this third battle, imagine a tree forging a letter V.

At **Yorktown**, the American army drove the Redcoats back to their ships, and the French Navy (on the side of the American colonists) prevented their escape. The surrender of General Cornwallis in October 19, 1781, was the last major battle of the war. *Four* rhymes with *door*. To remember this fourth battle, imagine the Empire State Building (in New York) with a giant door.

. . . .
IT'S YOUR TURN

Another way to remember a list is to make an acrostic. Take the first letters of the battles (L/C, S, V, and Y), and try to make a sentence using words that start with each letter. Be sure to keep the battles in order so you remember the order in which they happened.

The Federalist Papers

Alexander Hamilton, James Madison, and John Jay were among the writers of the Constitution. After they finished, the three published 85 articles in New York newspapers arguing in favor of its ratification by the states. These articles were called **The Federalist Papers.** They wrote under the name *Publius.*

The Federalist Papers are important to scholars because they explain what these writers of the Constitution intended.

You can use the first letters of their names to form an acrostic to help remember who wrote the Federalist Papers—and the respective amount that each wrote.

The **H**appily **M**ad **J**udge
Hamilton Madison Jay

Hamilton wrote the most, followed by **M**adison, and then **J**ay. Note that Mad is short for "Madison" and that John Jay was the first Chief Justice of the Supreme Court. (What a happy judge!)

Pretend you are Judge John Jay by putting on a bathrobe and jumping up and down in a victory celebration while chanting "I am the happily mad judge!"

Manifest Destiny

▶ "Mani-Feast Destiny"

Manifest Destiny was the nineteenth-century belief that the United States was destined to take over all the land up to the Pacific Ocean.

The end of *manifest* sounds like "feast," which means to eat as much food as you can.

The next time you're sitting at the dinner table and you're about to dig in, scream "Mani-feast Destiny!" and then greedily devour your dinner like it's your natural right to eat it all.

The Cherokees under Andrew Jackson's Democracy

▶ Andrew Jackson's new democracy,
did not apply to the Cherokee.
And it only got worse over the years,
with tragedies like the Trail of Tears.

Andrew Jackson, the seventh president of the United States, was very popular for being a man of the people. His "new" democracy valued the public good and put the rights of the common man above the elite. Sadly, however, he did not consider the Cherokee and other Native Americans to be worthy of the same rights.

To expand U.S. territory, Jackson took every opportunity to force Native Americans to move farther west. He made Native Americans accept treaties that made it legal for the United States to take their land away. In 1832, the Supreme Court said that state governments could not make laws forcing the Cherokee people to leave. Jackson defied this ruling and organized federal troops to force the **Cherokee** out of Georgia. The Cherokee marched hundreds of miles west along what is known as the **Trail of Tears.** Many of them died along the way. Jackson's disregard for the rights and the lives of Native Americans had terrible long-term effects, including war.

❝*Get This . . .*

Did you know that, just like there are rules of the road, there are also rules for boating? People who sail boats use rhyming mnemonics to remember some of these rules. Boaters must know who has the right of way if two boats are approaching each other, so that they don't collide. They also need to understand the system of different-colored lights that boats use to communicate at night. For example, if a boat is displaying one red light over another red light, it means that the boat is unattended. This might mean that the captain is sleeping, or it could mean that the boat is anchored. To remember what two red lights mean, captains use the mnemonic "Red over red, this boat is dead," or "Red over red, captain's in bed." **❞**

The Expansion of the United States

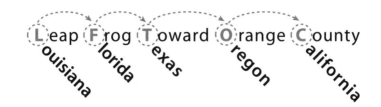

Leap Frog Toward Orange County
Louisiana Florida Texas Oregon California

In the nineteenth century, the United States expanded rapidly westward. In 1803, Thomas Jefferson completed the **Louisiana Purchase.** In 1819, the country acquired **Florida** from Spain in the Transcontinental Treaty. In 1845, **Texas** became a state after James Polk signed legislation to annex the territory. In 1846, Great Britain ceded the **Oregon Territory.** And, in 1850, **California** became a state, following the Mexican Revolution.

You can remember the order of the acquisitions with an acrostic "**L**eap **F**rog **T**oward **O**range **C**ounty." Each first letter of the acrostic stands for the large territory that the country gained, in chronological order. In case you don't know, Orange County is a large county in southern California. And for the first half of the nineteenth century, America *did* leap frog toward the OC!

Play a game of "Leap Frog" with a friend (jumping over each other's backs). With each jump, you should say each word of the acrostic—with your friend saying the corresponding territory that starts with the same letter.

Events Leading to the Civil War

▶ SWAB the DECK

Many different events led to the **U.S. Civil War.** Some laws that were passed by the federal government angered the North or the South. Violent acts between the North and the South increased the tension between the two regions. The capital letters in the acronym SWAB the DECK stand for eight events that eventually led to the Civil War.

Note that the word *the* is only included so that the mnemonic makes sense. Sailors on a ship are often ordered to "swab the deck." This means that they are supposed to clean the floor of the ship.

The following are eight events that led to the Civil War.

- **S**umner was caned: Charles Sumner, a Massachusetts senator, was attacked in the Senate in 1856 for speaking out against proslavery radicals.

- **W**ilmot Proviso: This proposed law would have outlawed slavery in any new territories, but it was never passed.

- **A**ttack on Harper's Ferry: John Brown attacked the Harper's Ferry arsenal in 1859 in a failed attempt to give guns to slaves for their eventual independence.

- **"B**leeding Kansas": From the mid- to late-1850s, the Kansas territory was the scene of a mini civil war over the issue of slavery.

- *D***red Scott v. Sandford**: This Supreme Court decision infuriated abolitionists by saying that slaves were not citizens.

- **E**lection of 1860: When Abraham Lincoln was elected president, it was the last straw for Southern states, who then decided to secede.

- **C**ompromise of 1850: This agreement, which intended to maintain a balance of free and slave states, related to the status of California and future western territories.

- **K**ansas-Nebraska Act: This 1854 act put an end to the Missouri Compromise and opened the way for future territories to become slave states.

IT'S YOUR TURN

Write the acronym SWAB the DECK on a piece of paper. After studying the list, see how many key events you can name based on the first letter of each one. While the word *civil* in "Civil War" means "about citizens," the word *civil* also means "polite." So you could imagine that a civil war should be fought on a clean surface. In order for that to happen, people would have to SWAB the DECK!

Reconstruction Amendments

▶ Ten-three, everybody goes **free**!
Ten-four, **citizen**ship galore!
Ten-five, **male voters** get to thrive!

Three amendments were ratified during the era in American history known as Reconstruction (1865–1877). At that time the federal government was trying to put the country back together after the Civil War. As a result, Congress passed laws and ratified these amendments to recognize the rights of African-Americans.

Each rhyme in the mnemonic reveals the importance of each amendment to the Constitution. The numbers correspond to the number of the amendment. The **13th Amendment** (ten-three) abolished slavery; the **14th Amendment** (ten-four) gave citizenship to every person born in the United States, as well as other rights; the **15th Amendment** (ten-five) gave black men (but not women of any color) the right to vote.

These three amendments insured or protected many freedoms. You can also remember this by thinking about how teenagers (aged 13, 14, and 15) begin to get more freedom from their parents and society.

Repeat the rhymes in this mnemonic like a mantra in your head. Repeat it over and over until it gets stuck in your brain and annoys anyone around you.

P. T. Barnum

P. T. Barnum was the best-known showman of the nineteenth century. His exhibitions spread across the range of popular amusements.

▶ In 1841, he opened his first **American Museum** in Manhattan. He filled it with highly dubious artifacts, such as the so-called bones of the Fiji Mermaid. *One* rhymes with *bun*. To remember Barnum's first major exhibit, imagine a bun on display in a museum.

Then, in 1850, he staged sold-out cross-country tours with the opera singer Jenny Lind, known as the **Swedish Nightingale**. *Two* rhymes with *shoe*. To remember Barnum's second major exhibit, imagine a bird making a nest in a shoe.

After coming out of retirement in 1871, Barnum founded his Greatest Show on Earth, which lives on as **Ringling Bros. and Barnum and Bailey Circus**. *Three* rhymes with *tree*. To remember Barnum's third major achievement, imagine a circus in a tree.

To remember the pegword associations, pretend you are P. T. Barnum and you have to get people into your shows. Be a showman! Sell the American Museum by telling people they will see the biggest bun in the world! Hawk the Swedish songbird by chirping loudly: "Kaw! Ka-kaw!" Convince potential customers to go to the circus by climbing into a tree and shouting down at them!

The Magnates of America

The term *magnate* originally was a title of nobility, particularly in the medieval times. But in the nineteenth century, it was used to describe the most powerful figures in American business.

At that time, several important **magnates** held all-controlling monopolies on various branches of industry. Three of the most important magnates are listed below the mnemonic.

▶ **"Magnate"** sounds like **"magnet."** A magnate is like a magnet and wields vast influence and draws money and power.

Andrew Carnegie (1835–1919) ran the steel industry. His mass production of steel rails revolutionized the railroads.

J.P. Morgan (1837–1913) owned banks and was a major player in the banking industry; you can still recognize his name in the banking and investment world today.

John D. Rockefeller (1839–1937) controlled the country's oil/petroleum industry, making himself at one point the richest man in America.

. . . .
IT'S YOUR TURN

Come up with ways to remember what each magnate controlled. You can remember that J.P. Morgan owned banks because Morgan sounds like "more" and you (almost) always want more money. You can also remember that John D. Rockefeller owned an oil company because he had to drill through rock to find it. How can you remember Andrew Carnegie?

The Golden Spike and the Transcontinental Railroad

▶ After the spike, no one had to hike.
By 1869, cross-country was fine.

After the Civil War, train companies raced to lay their tracks across the country to create a transcontinental railroad. The nation's newspapers covered the heated competition on their front pages. The Central Pacific hurdled east from California, while the Union Pacific sped west from Nebraska. In order to win, both companies overworked immigrant laborers from China and Ireland, as well as freed slaves and immigrants from other countries.

On **May 10, 1869,** in **Promontory Point,** Utah, the rail tracks met from the west met with the tracks from the east. Amid champagne toasts, the companies' chief engineers hammered in the golden spike, officially joining the lines.

You can use this rhyme to remember the completion of the transcontinental railroad was completed.

How many songs can you think of about trains? Try singing this mnemonic to their melodies. Come up with new lyrics for the songs using the facts above.

The Late Nineteenth-Century Strikes

Rapid industrialization and the rise of big business after the Civil War led to conflict with workers, who wanted better working conditions, better wages, and more control over their workplace. The three major strikes of the late nineteenth century (the Great Railroad Strike of 1877, the Homestead Strike of 1892, and the Pullman Strike of 1894) all failed, which shows the power of big business at the time.

▶ **The Great Railroad Strike of 1877** was the first major strike in the railroad industry. Employees of B&O Railroad called for it in response to receiving two pay cuts. President Hayes used federal troops to reopen the railroads. *One* rhymes with *bun*. To remember this first strike, imagine a train (#77) pulling a bun.

The Homestead Strike of 1892 was marked by a bloody battle between strikers and strike-breaking company guards (often called "Pinkertons") to Andrew Carnegie's steelworks. Several people died, and the strikers' defeat at the hands of Carnegie's company set back the unionization of steelworkers for decades. *Two* rhymes with *shoe*. To remember this second important strike, imagine a house (#92) in the shape of a shoe.

The Pullman Strike of 1894 was initiated by the American Railway Union in response to a 25 percent cut in wages by the Pullman Palace Car Company. Employees were on strike for three months, but President Grover Cleveland ordered troops to restore service to the rail yard, ending the strike within days. *Three* rhymes with *tree*. To remember this third important strike, imagine a man pulling (*Pull, man!*) on a tree.

The supremacy of the railroads and iron and steel manufacturing companies chugged along.

 To help you remember what each strike was about, draw your own picture of a train pulling something made out of iron or steel.

The Spanish-American War

▶ In **1898**, **Teddy Roosevelt** was the **main** man. After he climbed up a **hill**, he lit a **Cuban** cigar and chewed a piece of **gum**, and he saw all the way to the **Philippines**.

The Spanish-American War began in **1898** after the American naval ship, the USS *Maine*, exploded in Havana, Cuba. The United States accused Spain of blowing up the *Maine* (it blew up and sank by accident) and declared war.

During this short (and lopsided) war, **Teddy Roosevelt** led a successful attack against the Spanish on **San Juan Hill** in **Cuba,** which later helped him win the presidential election in 1904. As a result of the victory over Spain, the United States gained Puerto Rico and **Guam.** The United States also purchased the **Philippines** from Spain, thus becoming a legitimate overseas empire.

You can remember the main events of the Spanish American War by chaining a keyword in each event. You can think, "In 1898, Teddy Roosevelt was the main man" and remember that the ship, the USS *Maine*, exploded in 1898. You can also think, "After we climbed a hill" represents the San Juan Hill; "he lit a Cuban cigar" represents Cuba; "chewed a piece of gum" represents Guam; and "he saw all the way to the Philippines" represents the United States purchase of the Philippines.

Re-enact the sentence by acting out the actions in the chain. For example, grab a teddy bear and a map of Maine, and jump on your bed to represent charging up the hill. Pretend to smoke a Cuban cigar, chew a piece of gum, and imagine you're looking all the way to a distant place like the Philippines, an island nation in Asia.

Calvin Coolidge and
Laissez-Faire Economics

▶ "Let's say ... fair!"

Have you ever heard the expression "All's fair in love and war"? Well, in laissez-faire economics, all's fair in business too. **Laissez-faire** (lā´-sā´-fer) is a French term that basically means "let them do what they want." The key phrase "Let's say ... fair!" sound similar to the pronunciation of laissez-faire. They also express the way **President Calvin Coolidge** (1923–1929) believed the government should handle business in the United States.

Coolidge believed that businesses should be left to their own controls without government interference. Coolidge felt that business was designed to benefit the community it existed in. If there were any complaints about unfair business practices, Coolidge's response was that it *was* fair and that things would work themselves out.

In the late 1920s, business in the United States did prosper greatly, but not for everyone. Farmers were producing too much extra food. They couldn't sell it all and had to accept low prices for what they did sell. When the Congress tried to pass a law that would help out the farmers, Coolidge vetoed it. He felt that what the farmers were going through was a fair and natural part of capitalism. Many people believe that this philosophy led to the Great Depression in the United States.

Imagine that you are Calvin Coolidge. (You might want to hold an ice cube in your hands so you can stay *Cool*-idge.) Have a friend present a list of complaints about unfair business practices. For each complaint on the list, they should stop and ask you, the president, whether that business practice is fair or unfair. Respond in your best presidential accent, "Hmm, let's say ... fair!" For example, your friend might say, "John Rockefeller owns all the oil, so he is able to charge very high prices. Is this fair or unfair?" You know how to respond.

Causes of the Depression

▶ I bought a new sports car on Saturday with a **loan** from the dealer. I sped down the road, faster than I should have, really, so I didn't have time to avoid the full **produce** cart in the middle of the road. I **crashed** into the produce cart! **Dust** and fruit flew everywhere. The crash made me late for work, and my boss fired me. Now I'm **unemployed** and I **can't pay off my loan.** How **depressing**!

The Great Depression marked a traumatic era in the history of not only the United States but the world. Starting officially in 1929 (and lasting until about 1939), the Great Depression was tied to human suffering and a complete overhaul of economic policy.

The Great Depression was precipitated by an unfortunate coincidence of factors. Too many people were purchasing goods through **loans** and businesses were **overproducing** goods that not enough people could buy. When the market **crashed** in October 1929, stock owners could **no longer make payments on their loans.**

In the early 1930s, a drought in the Midwest left the soil dry. The wind kicked up giant dust storms, causing massive erosion and giving rise to the term *Dust Bowl*. Many farmers lost everything, and the lack of crops raised food prices. Many starved.

Banks, suddenly without capital to operate, had to close, and many businesses folded, causing massive **unemployment.** (Up to a third of the nation was unemployed during the Great Depression.)

To remember the events that transpired to make the Great Depression the most devastating economic depression, use a chain of events that create a memorable story for you. The car crash into the produce stand is one such example.

It's Your Turn

The Great Depression also led to an enormous change in government. Many of the programs we take for granted today were started by President Franklin Roosevelt during this time. Try to add any or all of these Depression-era programs to your chaining mnemonic: the Securities Exchange Commission, the Federal Reserve, the Social Security Administration, and the Tennessee Valley Authority. Some programs didn't survive, but have left their mark. Look up the Works Progress Administration and the Civilian Conservation Corps, for example.

The First Atomic Bombs

During World War II, American scientists researched atomic weapons—the most powerful, destructive, and dangerous weapon known to humankind at the time. In 1945, they detonated the world's first three nuclear bombs. The **Manhattan Project,** a group working for the U.S. government in the New Mexico desert, dropped the first on July 16th, 1945.

The Air Force dropped the second atomic bomb—nicknamed **"Little Boy"**—on the Japanese city of Hiroshima on August 6th. U.S. pilots dropped the third atomic bomb—called **"Fat Man"**—on another Japanese city, Nagasaki, on August 9th.

The two nuclear blasts in Japan killed approximately 110,000 Japanese civilians and wounded countless others. The bombs caused the Japanese to surrender to the United States less than a week after the dropping of "Fat Man" on Nagasaki, ending World War II. Historians and citizens alike continue to debate the choice to use the destructive and deadly weapon.

▶ You can remember the names of these first three atomic bombs by using the pegword method. Simply devise a mnemonic for each of the three names with the three corresponding pegwords—bun, shoe, and tree. For the Manhattan Project, you can consider an element of Manhattan—say, the Empire State Building—holding together two buns in a sandwich. For Little Boy, think about a small child wearing shoes that are way too big for him. And for Fat Man, you can place an obese guy in the branches of a tree, which are causing the limbs to strain and bend.

A personal memory will create a better way to remember. If you can connect personal feelings and experiences to the information—the world's first atomic bombs—you'll have a much better chance to remember the details.

1950s Civil Rights Milestones

▶ Mr. **Brown** played **board** games at the **park** with his friend **Rose**, who would always shout "**King** me!"

By the mid-1950s, the modern Civil Rights Movement was gaining momentum. In *Brown v. Board of Education of Topeka* (1954), the Supreme Court ordered the desegregation of public schools. In 1955, **Rosa Parks** launched the **Montgomery Bus boycott**, which led to the desegregation of public services. In 1957, **Martin Luther King, Jr.** was appointed leader of the Southern Christian Leadership Conference, which organized many protests during the Civil Rights Movement.

Mr. Brown, the father of a child who went to a segregated school, won the Supreme Court case against the Kansas Board of Education. Rosa Parks refused to give up her seat to a white man on a segregated bus in Montgomery, Alabama. She was arrested, which sparked the bus boycott.

Chaining the key civil rights milestones in chronological order—**Brown** and **board** for *Brown v. the Board of Education of Topeka*, **park** and **Rose** for Rosa Parks, and **King** to represent Martin Luther King, Jr.—will help you remember the order of these pivotal milestones in the early Civil Rights Movement.

Say the sentence out loud so you can hear it as well as imagine it. Picture a woman named Rose playing a board game (checkers) and saying "King me!" Shout it yourself for good measure.

Henry Kissinger: An American Statesman

▶ "KISSinger" and make up!

In 1968, President Nixon appointed **Henry Kissinger** as his national security adviser. He later served as Secretary of State. Kissinger was a successful diplomat, and he made great strides toward making peace between the United States and several communist countries, including North Vietnam, the Soviet Union, and China.

Kissinger won a Nobel Peace Prize in 1973 for his involvement in negotiating an end to the Vietnam War. In addition, he is credited for relaxing Cold War tensions between the United States and the Soviet Union throughout the 1970s. Finally, Kissinger paved the way for Nixon to visit and speak with the leader of China. This one visit had an enormous effect on the United States and the rest of the world. China agreed to keep diplomatic talks open and also agreed to begin trading with the United States.

Repeat the keyword phrase *loudly* many times. Eventually, your parents may ask you what on earth you are doing! Won't they be impressed when you ask them if they're aware of how important a figure Henry Kissinger was? Tell them that Kissinger laid the first planks of the bridge toward peace with communist countries. Next, ask them if they can do an impression of Henry Kissinger so that you will know what he sounded like. They probably can't match how deep and raspy Kissinger's voice is, but it's fun to hear them try!

Cold War Crises of the Kennedy Administration

The **Cold War** was the period of hostility between communist countries and non-communist Western countries that lasted from the end of World War II to about 1989. During John F. Kennedy's presidency, there were three main events that symbolized the continuing conflict between the United States and the world's communist nations. Each of these events was a crisis that threatened to escalate the tensions to an all-out war.

▶ The first crisis was the **Bay of Pigs** invasion in April 1961. It was an invasion by U.S. troops designed to overthrow Fidel Castro. Castro was the communist leader of Cuba. The invasion failed, and tensions between the United States and the Soviet Union, a communist ally of Cuba, increased. *One* rhymes with *bun*. To remember this first main event of the Cold War, imagine a pig on a boat biting on a bun.

This led to the second crisis. Because the United States was clearly willing to launch attacks against communism, the Soviet Union decided to block off the communist area of East Germany.

In August 1961, the Soviet Union built the **Berlin Wall**, separating East Berlin from West Berlin. This move also prevented East Germans who did not want to live under communist rule from escaping. *Two* rhymes with *shoe*. To remember this second main event of the Cold War, imagine a wall made of shoes.

The third crisis of the Cold War during Kennedy's presidency was the **Cuban missile crisis**. Castro had asked the Soviet Union for more weapons to defend against America. Kennedy ordered a blockade to stop Soviet ships from delivering missiles to Cuba. The Soviets agreed to turn back, but only after the United States promised not to invade Cuba again. *Three* rhymes with *tree*. To remember this third main event of the Cold War, imagine a tree bristling with missiles.

Repeat the pegwords in this mnemonic along with the name of the crisis each one stands for. For example, you could repeat the following phrases: "*One* rhymes with *bun*. A pig eating a bun tells me the Bay of Pigs invasion came first. *Two* rhymes with *shoe*. A wall made of shoes tells me the construction of the Berlin Wall came second. *Three* rhymes with *tree*. A tree full of missiles tells me that the Cuban missile crisis came third."

The Order of the Presidents

▶ **W**ashington's **A**rmy **J**ogged **M**any **M**iles **A**nd **J**ogged **V**ery **H**ard **T**o **P**hiladelphia **T**o **F**ind **P**atriotic, **B**asic **L**iberty.

This mnemonic won't tell you the names of the presidents, but it will help you establish the order up to Honest Abe. And if you know the names of the presidents but can't remember their order, this lengthy acrostic can point you in the right direction!

The first letter of each word in the sixteen-word sentence tells you the first letter of the first sixteen presidents. In order, those presidents are as follows:

George **W**ashington (1789–1797)
John **A**dams (1797–1801)
Thomas **J**efferson (1801–1809)
James **M**adison (1809–1817)
James **M**onroe (1817–1825)
John Quincy **A**dams (1825–1829)
Andrew **J**ackson (1829–1837)
Martin **V**an Buren (1837–1841)
William Henry **H**arrison (1841)
John **T**yler (1841–1845)
James **P**olk (1845–1849)
Zachary **T**aylor (1849–1850)
Millard **F**illmore (1850–1853)
Franklin **P**ierce (1853–1857)
James **B**uchanan (1857–1861)
Abraham **L**incoln (1861–1865)

IT'S YOUR TURN

What else could Washington's Army have jogged many miles to Philadelphia for besides "Patriotic, Basic Liberty"? Peanut Butter Lollipops? Come up with your own twist to the mnemonic if it will make it more personal for you?

Also, you can use this type of mnemonic to remember the order of *all* the presidents. You can chunk the presidents into smaller groups to make smaller acrostics. For example, the mnemonic on this page goes from the start of the country through the Civil War. You could make your own acrostic with the presidents from Reconstruction through World War I, then another from World War I through the present. Visit www.whitehouse.gov/ history/presidents for an up-to-date list of the presidents.

The Gulf of Tonkin Resolution

In the summer of 1964, North Vietnamese torpedo boats supposedly began firing on United States' vessels in the **Gulf of Tonkin**, between Vietnam and China. It was unclear at the time (and still is, to some degree) if the attacks were in fact launched by the Vietnamese. Nonetheless, President Lyndon B. Johnson used them as an excuse to escalate the United States' military involvement in Asia. The Gulf of Tonkin Incident marked the official involvement of the United States in the Vietnam War.

▶ "Tonkin" sounds like "honkin'," the sound a general might make with his tank while impatiently waiting to invade a country. So, to remember this important turning point in the Vietnam War, just imagine an anxious **LBJ honkin'** on the horn while preparing to attack in the **Gulf of Tonkin**.

 Honk the horn of your imaginary tank and declare repeatedly that you are "honkin' for Tonkin." Then scream and charge. Water balloons help.

Congress

The United States legislature, also known as **Congress,** is our country's law-making body. The U.S. Congress has two separate houses: the Senate and the House of Representatives. In order for a bill to be passed, it has to be approved by both houses.

The U.S. **Senate** has **100 members,** 2 from each state. The vice-president is the official leader of the Senate and has the power to cast a tie-breaking vote. The Senate has the power to impeach government officials (charge them with a crime). The Senate also has the power to approve cabinet appointments, Supreme Court nominees, and treaties. A senator serves a **six-year term** and must be at least **thirty years old** to be elected. You can remember the number of senators with the following mnemonic.

▶ There are 100 cents in a dollar. And there are 100 "cents"-ators in the senate.

The **House of Representatives** has **435 members,** and each member represents a certain district. Representatives are supposed to voice the views of the people they represent, who are known as their *constituents.* The number of representatives a state is based on its population. California has fifty-three representatives, while tiny Rhode Island has just two. A member of the House of Representatives serves a **two-year term** and must be at least **twenty-five years old** to be elected.

To remember the number of representatives in the House, use the following mnemonic.

▶ The representatives of my state asked me for a contribution. So I reached into my wallet **for three five**-dollar bills.

❝*Get This . . .*

The number of representatives in the House of Representatives changes as the population changes in the United States. After the census is held at the end of each decade, the number of representatives changes accordingly. You might have to change this mnemonic in 2011! **❞**

The Stock Market

► Bulls are full, but the bears all swear.

When investors purchases securities or commodities and stock values rise, they refer to it as a **bullish market.** When investors over-excitedly sell their goods and prices drop, they call it a **bearish market.**

In case you were wondering, the terms' origins are European. "Don't sell the bearskin before you've killed the bear," warns the old French proverb to overexcited businessmen. The "bull market" likely derives from a grizzly bloodsport from seventeenth-century England known as "bull baiting," in which bulldogs attacked tethered bulls.

Use the rhyme to remember what each animal represents.

A bull's horns point up, so you can connect the image of a bull's horns with that of stocks going up. Bears attack their pray with their claws, which point down; you can connect that visual image with that of stocks going down.

Types of Protest

During the 1950s and 1960s, many people participated in forms of non-violent protest. They demonstrated to support civil rights, to oppose the Vietnam War, and to support a host of other causes. Many, like Dr. Martin Luther King, Jr., organized vast marches. Others, like Bob Dylan, composed political folk songs. Some took part in group organizations, such as sit-ins to protest the segregation of lunch counters in the South. Many practiced peaceful resistance, where they refused to fight the police who arrested them.

▶ Create flash cards to remember the different ways you can protest.

- Make a "march" card and put it by your shoes.
- Make a "political song" card and put it by your stereo.
- Tape "sit-in" cards to the back of every chair in the house.
- Put a "peaceful resistance" card on a doll or teddy bear.

Take a stand for what you believe in! Try out some of these techniques. Get your family involved. March to support a local cause or practice peaceful resistance by signing petitions and choosing not to purchase goods from companies you don't support.

Does your math teacher like to give tests every day? (Is he or she *protest*?) Write a song about how unfair it is. (We don't recommend resistance when it comes to taking an exam, though.)

Lobbying

Lobbyists are private citizens who attempt to influence the government's decisions. There are several different types of lobbyists. **Grassroots lobbyists** try to effect change by getting the public involved through local campaigns. The hope is that people will then voice their concerns in great numbers and the government will listen.

Public interest groups are organizations that attempt to protect the public by ensuring that the government is acting in their best interests. For example, a public interest group may act as a watchdog for environmental issues, or it may advocate on behalf of consumers.

A company might hire **corporate lobbyists** to convince the government to pass laws that will benefit that company. For example, advocates for pharmaceutical corporations may lobby Congress for legislation that will make it easier to get a new drug approved.

Various lobbying groups pay **think tanks** to do their research for them. A think tank is a privately funded (usually) research group, comprised of academics or experts in a field, that attempts to shape government policy, among other roles. Think tanks often have strong partisan leanings with "findings" that support a particular ideology.

▶ Create a series of four flash cards for each different element of lobbying.

- Make a "grassroots" card and put it in front of a potted plant (or in your front yard!).
- A "public interest group" can go atop a clipboard or notepad.
- A "corporate" card can go on top of a jar of pennies or wallet.
- A card for "think tank" can go in front of a clear bowl or fish tank.

Arrange all of these items in the "lobby" of your house. Pretend you are a senator and all of them are trying to give you money to pass a bill. Argue with them at length. Persuade your mother's petunias that they are wrong.

The Neolithic Revolution

The Neolithic Revolution was the period of human development characterized by permanent settlements of people, occurring approximately 15,000–20,000 years ago. Several transformations took place during this historical era at the end of the Stone Age.

As people began to harvest crops **(agriculture)** and domesticate livestock **(animal domestication),** they began to settle down **(sedentary),** causing a growth in human population. And as more people stayed in one place, small-scale **governments** began to take hold. **Organized religion** also emerged, and with it, the influence of religious leaders. There was also a rise in local and long distance **trade,** as the settled people needed goods not produced near their homes.

▶ Create a series of six flash cards for each important transformation that took place during the Neolithic Revolution.

- Make an "agriculture" card and put it in front of a slice of bread.
- For "animal domestication," put a card in front of a glass of milk.
- A card named "sedentary" can go on your bed. (Your bed pretty much stays in one place, right?)
- For "government," put a card in front of a driver's license, learner's permit, passport, or a student ID card.
- For "organized religion," put a card in front of a bible or other sacred book. (If you don't have one, perhaps put it by a candle.)
- A card for "trade" can go by a piece of jewelry. (If you trade baseball cards or something similar, that would work too!)

You can also get creative with where you put the cards. Just make sure they represent each element. If a cheeseburger will help you remember both the domestication of plants (the bun) and of animals (the beef), then put the agriculture and animal domestication cards by a cheeseburger. Just don't eat the cards.

Walk around your home to each of the cards. Act like it's 8000 B.C., and you're finally settling down after millennia as a nomad in the Stone Age.

The Cradles of Civilization

There were four major river valleys where human civilizations first arose. The **Tigris-Euphrates** rivers were found in Mesopotamia, now modern-day Iraq. The **Indus River** ran through India and formed that cradle of civilization. The **Nile** is famous for helping civilization form in Africa—specifically in the region near Egypt. The **Yellow River** (also called the Huang He or Huang Ho) formed the Chinese cradle of civilization. If you use the first letter of each river valley, you will spell the acronym TINY.

Tigres-Euphrates

Indus

Nile

Yellow

Heavy rains caused each of these rivers to flood annually. When the waters receded, the silt (or dirt) left behind was rich in nutrients for plants. It is theorized that human nomads noticed seeds grew easily in the silt, and thus, farming was born. Farming formed the foundation for modern civilization.

The acronym TINY is particularly helpful because the human population of the world at that time was a very small fraction of what it is today.

If you remember better with colors, you can easily associate the names of the rivers with like colors. Get some colored pencils and a blank sheet of paper.

Write Yellow River with a yellow pencil. Tigris sounds a bit like tiger. Write Tigris-Euphrates using orange and black pencils, like the colors of a tiger. Indus sounds like Indigo, so write this word in dark blue. And the Nile, well, you could say it sounds like violet. Or maybe you know that it runs parallel to the Red Sea. When you think of these rivers, think of the colors to help you remember the names.

Ancient Roman Achievements

All Roads Lead to Rome.

Aqueducts Roads Law Republic

Whereas the Greeks advanced civilization through abstract ideas in Plato's *Republic*, the Romans pushed forward by means of engineering and applied science. The accomplishments of the successful empire are still considered some of the world's greatest feats today. To recall some of the more impressive feats, use the famous expression "All Roads Lead to Rome." The first letter of each word stands for a remarkable achievement.

Aqueducts brought water to Rome in a true feat of architectural marvel. For more than 500 years, the Romans built hundred of miles of aqueducts, carrying water from as far away as 57 miles—sometimes over valleys on stone arches. Some of these aqueducts are still in use today!

The Romans built **roads** and bridges to direct all manner of trade goods and people from every part of the Empire. There is a reason that the "All Roads Lead to Rome" expression is so well known!

A uniform set of written **laws** governed the entire populace of Rome. In fact, the Roman law helped form the foundation for most of the development of law in the Western world.

Tyrannical king Tarquin was ousted in 509 B.C., ending the reign of the monarchy in Rome, and marking the start of Rome's **Republic**. For the next several centuries, the Roman state grew, and the Republic's institutions adapted accordingly. By the time of the collapse of the Republic, with the assassination of Julius Caesar, the Republic had taken huge leaps in advancements of culture, economics, and government. In fact, the term *senator* (see page 122) comes from Rome.

In order to depict Rome for the movie *Gladiator*, artists and historians worked together to develop a computer simulation of the city itself. Though much in the movie is fiction, this rendering is considered excellent. Rent the movie and take a look at the thriving metropolis that was ancient Rome.

Mesoamerican Civilizations

▶ **O**ffensive
Conquistadors
Mistook
The
Americas as
India

There were several major Mesoamerican civilizations before the arrival of Europeans in the early 16th century. The **Olmecs**, **Maya**, **Toltecs**, and **Aztecs** were all located in what is now mainly Mexico, while the Chavín and Inca were located in the Andes mountain range and along the western coast of South America.

The **Olmec** made their initial marks on the continent at about 1150 B.C. and disappeared at about 800 B.C.

The **Chavín** culture prospered largely between 900 B.C. and 200 B.C., although their people had lived for many centuries beforehand.

Although the **Maya** civilization may have developed as early as 1500 B.C., its impressive rise to prominence began in 250 A.D. and lasted until about 900 A.D.—an era of Mayan culture that is referred to as the Classic Period.

The **Toltec** civilization dominated their region of Mexico from roughly 900 A.D. to about 1200 A.D.

Both the **Aztec** and the **Inca** civilizations ruled large areas, intensifying their powers in the early 1400s. Both empires fell to the Spanish explorers—the Aztecs in 1521 and the Incas by 1535.

To remember the names and loose order of each Mesoamerican civilization, you can use the first letter of each to form an acrostic. Note that the conquistadors were the Spanish explorers and soldiers who conquered and colonized the Americas. These early explorers initially mistook the Americas as India—and thus named the region the Indies and its inhabitants Indians.

. . . .
It's Your Turn

Make your own acrostic given the rough O-C-M-T-A-I order of Mesoamerican civilizations. Here are a few places to start:
Other Children . . .
Of Course . . .
Orange Crayons . . .

Martin Luther and the Reformation

▶ Hey, do you want to **indulge** in something gross? Take a **15**-to-**17** minute trip to the café. Gather your **wits** and get on I-**95**. Make a right at the **Lutheran Church**. The church will be **closed**, so you won't see any **priests**. But have **faith**, you'll be almost there. Walk a little farther down the sidewalk and you'll see a café serving **worms**.

The Catholic Church was the only Christian church until the end of the Middle Ages. Among the most outrageous abuses in the eyes of some priests at the time was the selling of **indulgences**—rich men could pay money to the church and receive pardon for their sins.

A German monk saw this as only one of many problems with the church. In **1517**, he walked to his nearby church in **Wittenburg** and nailed a document listing 95 reforms needed with the church, called his **95 Theses**. The author was named **Martin Luther.**

Ultimately, Luther had three basic principles: The Bible was the ultimate source of religion, not the **church**; individuals had a personal relationship with God, and **priests** were not required; and **faith**—not good works—is enough to be a pious man.

Luther was summoned before the assembly, known to history as the **Diet of Worms** (since it was in the city of Worms in Germany). Luther refused to back down and had to go into hiding to protect his own safety. But the damage was done. The church divided.

These ideas sparked a massive revolt and divide against and within the church leading to the many sects of Christianity there are today.

You can use this mnemonic to remember the information involving Martin Luther and the Reformation of the Catholic Church.

. . . .
It's Your Turn

Try to make your own story that will help you remember the chain of events involved with this important religious turning point. You don't have to fit everything in, but the more the merrier.

West African Empires

▶ **Golly, Molly,** you can **sing**! You're as good as **gold**!

Ghana, Mali, and **Songhai** were the three largest empires of West Africa. They all got rich from the trans-Saharan trade networks that linked West Africa to the Mediterranean and to the Middle East. The control of the **gold** trade was essential to the wealth of these empires, especially for Ghana and Mali.

In this mnemonic, **Golly** stands for Ghana. The two words sound alike and even have the same number of syllables. Then, the word **Molly** stands for Mali. The two words begin with the same letter and have similar vowel sounds. Note also that the word **sing** sounds a lot like Songhai—the word *song* (something you would sing) is even a part of the word *Songhai*.

The repetition of the hard *g* sound in the second sentence reinforces the keyword "gold," the most important resource for these West African empires.

Pretend you're a famous singer named Molly (maybe even Molly Golly), and sing like you're creating gold records. It will help you remember what you're doing if you can pretend like you're from one of the ancient empires of western Africa. When you're done, make sure you say the mnemonic for these West African empires out loud. You may want to do this in a place where no one can hear you.

Causes of World War I

Militarism
Alliance
Imperialism
Nationalism

The acronym MAIN is a useful way of remembering the four primary factors that led to World War I.

Militarism (the idea that a country should have a strong army and navy): Germany was building up its military and Britain, who had traditionally had the strongest navy in the world, was feeling threatened.

Alliances (nations pledging support to each other, bound by their common distrust of other countries): Since almost every nation had multiple alliances, any conflict was bound to become a worldwide affair. Leading up to World War I, the two main alliances were the Triple Alliance (Italy, Germany, and Austria-Hungary) and the Triple Entente (Great Britain, France, and Russia).

Imperialism (the idea that a powerful country should control smaller, weaker regions): The decline of the Ottoman Empire opened up the East to colonization and European countries fought over African colonies too.

Nationalism (the idea that one's country is the best in the world and is worth fighting for): The Serbians wanted a Slavic national identity separate from Austro-Hungarian rule. After having lost territory in the Franco-Prussian War, the French nationalists wanted revenge. And the founding of the German Empire had created a strong sense of national pride among Germans.

To remember that the acronym MAIN stands for the causes of World War I, remember that World War I was one of the *main* events of the twentieth century for almost every world power. It was even called the Great War and the "war to end all wars," although of course we now know that wasn't true. To help you understand the impact of this war, consider that over 15 million people lost their lives.

 Write the acronym MAIN on a piece of paper, and then write each major factor that led to World War I using the first letter of the acronym.

The History of Telecommunications

In the nineteenth century, there were several important breakthroughs in telecommunications.

In 1820, Danish scientist **Hans Christian Oersted** discovered the electrical process used to create the **telegraph.**

In the early to mid–1830s, **Samuel Morse** built the first electrical telegraph. Several years later, he created **Morse Code,** a language of dots and dashes used by telegraph operators.

In 1876, **Alexander Graham Bell** invented the **telephone.** (He was trying to build what he called a "harmonic telegraph.")

You can remember the names of these inventors, and the order of their innovations, by chaining their names (and using keywords that *sound* like their names).

▶ **Instead** of a **horse**, ring the **bells**!

"Instead" sounds like "Oerstead," and "horse" sounds like "Morse." "Bells" isn't too far off from "Bell," either. These three inventors allowed people to communicate even if they were far away from one another (ringing bells), instead of having to be face-to-face (such as carrying messages to neighboring towns by horseback).

 Find a bell in your home, and ring it loud. As you do, say aloud "Instead of a horse, ring the bells! Oersted of a Morse, ring the Bell!"

Scramble for Africa

The Scramble for Africa took place from the 1880s through the early part of the twentieth century, at the height of modern European imperialism. Several European states competed with each other to take control of as much African territory as they could.

The Europeans were able to conquer the interior of Africa only after discovering medicine like quinine, which treated and prevented malaria, a big tropical killer. Advances in weaponry, especially new types of rifles and early machine guns, also gave the Europeans a big advantage over the native Africans.

▶ Use the mnemonic on the previous page to recall how the soldiers "scrambled" for African land.

Note that the Scramble for Africa is also sometimes referred to as the Race for Africa.

Count how many soldiers are running toward Africa. This represents the major Europeans powers that sought to colonize Europe. Draw pictures on the continent itself that represent what attracted the Europeans to Africa (natural resources, competition for territory, etc.).

Events of the Early Cold War

Today Must Be Nearly Winter

The Cold War was the rivalry between the United States and Russia (and their respective allies) following the end of World War II in 1945. It was not a war fought with weapons, but rather with politics and economics. Several significant events transpired in the decade that followed.

The **Truman Doctrine** was declared by President Harry S Truman on March 12, 1947. It challenged Communist aggression by providing funds to countries (like Greece or Turkey) under perceived communist threat.

The United States' **Marshall Plan,** formed in April 1948, granted millions of dollars to Western Europeans states to help them rebuild after the war. Eastern Europe and the Soviet Union did not participate.

The **Berlin Airlift** air-delivered food and other essential supplies to the people of West Berlin after Stalin ordered the blockade of that city. Organized by the United States and Britain, it began in June 1948 and continued through 1949.

The **North Atlantic Treaty Organization (NATO)** was formed by twelve countries on April 4, 1949, to form an alliance and oppose a possible Soviet invasion of Western Europe. (Other countries joined at later dates.)

The **Warsaw Pact** was formed by the Soviets as a counterpart to NATO in 1955. It originally formed a military alliance between eight countries under the soviet military.

The first letter of each word in the mnemonics corresponds to a key point in the early stages of the Cold War. Just think how *cold* it must be to say something like that.

Walk to your refrigerator and open the freezer door. Hold your face close to the cool blast, and close your eyes. Say out loud, "**T**oday **M**ust **B**e **N**early **W**inter!"

European Unity

During the late twentieth century, many countries in Europe agreed to work and trade together more easily. The European Coal and Steel Community, the Common Market, and the European Union helped unite the European continent.

The **European Coal and Steel Community** was an agency formed in 1952 to coordinate the production of two key resources (coal and steel, obviously) among Western European countries. Within a few years the ECSC had removed many trade barriers.

In 1957, the European Community (also known as the **Common Market**) was created in large part by the Treaty of Rome. When that went into action, internal tariffs disappeared, and the European Community (EC) acquired both judicial and taxing power.

In 1993, the European Community was renamed the **European Union,** featuring a common **currency** (the Euro), free competition, and the elimination of border controls among member countries.

Each progression of European unity included more and more of the European economy. The initial cooperation on coal and steel production went on to include virtually all aspects of the European economy. Also, many European countries have joined the European Union since its origins in the 1950s, including East European countries like Poland and the Czech Republic, who joined after the end of the Cold War.

▶ My first trip to Europe was really cool, and I got a steal while shopping for common goods at the market. I found the love of my life there! We got married, forming a union, and we even combined our money together.

This mnemonic connects the historical terms together in chronological order. "Cool and steal" represents the "Coal and Steel" Community. "Common" goods at the "market" refers to the Common Market. And the "union" included the merging of "money"—just like the Euro!

Connect the organizations, visually, such as with a triangle where each of the three sides represents the three major turning points in the history of European unity. Try to draw details that show how each organization was important for European unity.

The Five Pillars of Islam

▶ **P**ious **F**ollowers **A**chieve **F**ive **P**illars.

This acrostic helps you remember the **Five Pillars of Islam.** The Five Pillars of Islam are the different acts that Sunni Muslims must carry out. The first letter of each word in the acrostic stands for one of the Five Pillars of Islam. Remember that *pious* is another word for religious.

The Five Pillars of Islam are:

Prayer: Muslims must recite five daily prayers at specific times of day.

Faith: Muslims must proclaim a belief in God (Allah) and the prophet Muhammad.

Alms: Muslims must donate a certain percent of their savings to the poor.

Fasting: During the holy month of Ramadan, healthy, adult Muslims may not eat or drink from dawn to dusk.

Pilgrimage: Once in a lifetime, a Muslim should make a pilgrimage to the holy city of Mecca.

The fact that the words *Five Pillars* are part of the acrostic will help you remember the mnemonic. Also, the sentence actually describes something about the topic. It tells you that devoted Muslims follow the Five Pillars.

Another unique aspect of this acrostic is that the letters PFAFP form a palindrome. That means the letters are the same forward and backward. This can help you remember if you forget one of the words.

Major World Religions

▶ Jesus Comes Back (Jesus, Christianity, Bible)

 Muhammad Is Quick (Muhammad, Islam, Quran)

 Nobody Hates Vegetables (No major leader, Hindus, Vedas)

 Buddha Boils For Tea (Buddha, Buddhism, Four Truths)

 Moses Journeys To Israel (Moses, Judaism, Torah, Israel)

Christianity, Islam, Hindu, Buddhism, and Judaism are five of the world's major world religions. Each one has its own major text that forms the basis of the religion. Also, most of these religions had a major leader or founder. The five acrostics give you a way to remember the major religious leader, the religion, and the important religious text for the five most popular world religions. (The religions are listed in order from the greatest number of followers to the fewest.)

Note how each acrostic helps you remember one element about the religion as well:

- Christians believe Jesus was resurrected from the grave.
- Muhammad quickly conquered much of the known world.
- Hindus do not believe in eating meat.
- Buddha focuses on meditation (and some people find tea soothing and helpful for medication).
- The Jews believe Israel is their ancestral home and they were led there by Moses.

· · · · · · · · · · · · ·
IT'S YOUR TURN

There are more religions than just these five. Come up with an acrostic of your own to remember the major elements of another. (See page 130 to read about the foundations of Lutheran, for example.)

The Tropic of Cancer

▶ Raise your hand to answer,
where's the tropic of Cancer?

Many people confuse the tropic of Cancer and the tropic of Capricorn. The **tropic of Cancer** is an imaginary line that runs around the earth at about 23.27° north of the equator. It runs through Mexico, Egypt, and India. The tropic of Capricorn is the imaginary line that runs around the earth at about 23.27° south of the equator. It runs through Australia, Brazil, and South Africa.

The word *raise* in the rhyme will help you remember that the tropic of Cancer is *above* the equator. In the Northern Hemisphere, the sun is directly above the tropic of Cancer at noon on the first day of summer (around June 21).

· · · · · · · · · · · ·
IT'S YOUR TURN

One way to keep busy on long drives while brushing up on your geography skills is to play geography games such as "I'm thinking of a country that starts with the letter *A*." How many countries can you think of that begin with the letter *A*?

You can also look at a world map and see how many countries you can find whose names start with *A*. Use mnemonics to remember the names of unfamiliar countries. For example, you might imagine a celebrity shopping for *antiques* with body guards (*armed men*) to remember Antigua and Armenia. After you study the map and create a few of your own mnemonics, play the game with a friend. One person may start by naming Australia, and then the other person might reply with Angola. Keep going until one player is stumped.

Order of the Greater Scandinavian Countries

▶ **N**o
Smoking
Friend

The term *Scandinavia* generally refers to the countries of Norway, Sweden, and Denmark. But people often refer to the term *Greater Scandinavia*, which also includes neighboring Finland. Norway, Sweden, and Finland are the large countries at the northern section of the European continent. Use the acrostic above to remember their order from west to east.

Notice how the first letter in each word in the acrostic represents one on of these three countries. So, the **N** in **N**o represents Norway, the **S** in **S**moking represents Sweden, and the **F** in **F**riend represents Finland. This is also the geographical order of these countries, from west to east (or left to right on a map).

Denmark is the fourth country in Scandinavia. But it is on the European mainland, so it does not share any borders with Sweden, Norway, or Finland—so it is easier to locate. It is also much smaller than the other countries in Scandinavia.

❝Get This . . .

In June 2005 the entire country of Sweden banned smoking in all restaurants, cafes, bars, and nightclubs. Norway already had a smoking ban. Perhaps that can help you to remember the geography of the three large countries!❞

Longitude vs. Latitude

Longitude, latitude. Latitude, longitude. One means a distance north or south from the equator. The other means a distance east or west of the prime meridian. Put the two geographical terms together, and you can find any spot on the planet. But get them mixed up, and you might end up way, way off target. So, how can you remember which is which?

The two terms are spelled nearly alike. But one starts with "long" and the other starts with "lat." Look at the diagram of longitude and latitude on the following page.

The lines of longitude go from the North Pole to the South Pole. The lines of **longitude** are *always long*! The lines of latitude go from east to west. As they get closer to the poles, they decrease in length. The lines of latitude change size, depending on how far from the equator they are. Remember this, and you'll always remember that longitude lines are the consistently **long** lines on a map.

Some people get cranky when the weather gets too hot or too cold. If they flew north or south, maybe they could change their attitude. So you could say that they could change their **attitude** by changing their **latitude.** Remember this rhyme, and you'll always remember that longitude is the distance from the equator.

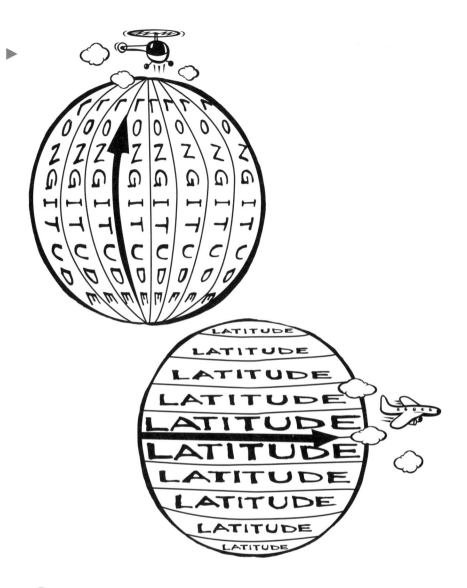

Say the words *longitude* and *latitude* out loud, stressing the *loooong* part of *longitude*. Use *latitude* in a sentence to a friend, associating it with a change in temperature.

State Capitals in New England

New England is the region in the northeastern United States that includes Maine, New Hampshire, Vermont, Massachusetts, Rhode Island, and Connecticut. Most people remember that Boston is the capital of Massachusetts, but they have trouble recalling some of the lesser-known New England state capitals.

That's where these mock bumper stickers come in. Have you ever read a silly bumper sticker—maybe something about whirled peas or honor students—and it has stuck in your head much longer than you would have liked? Well, we hope the bumper stickers on the following page will stick with you because they can help you remember your state capitals. For example, while "I 'hart' Connecticut" might seem like an egregious misspelling at first, in fact, it is intended to help you remember that Hartford is the capital of Connecticut.

The other state capitals represented by the bumper stickers are **Augusta, Maine; Concord, New Hampshire; Hartford, Connecticut;** and **Providence, Rhode Island** (although many people think that the entire state of Rhode Island is an island, most of the state is part of the mainland).

It's Your Turn

Draw a bumper sticker that could help someone remember the capital of the state in which you live. If you live in one of the New England states already shown, pick a state capital that you always forget and draw a bumper sticker that can help you remember in the future.

**Memorize 42,195 digits of pi—
or maybe just 10.**

Roman Numerals

▶ Ivy's **XL** Coat Disappoints Mary

The Roman numeral system uses the letters I, V, X, L, C, D, and M to represent numbers. This is very different from the usual Arabic numeral system, which uses numbers we're more familiar with: 0, 1, 2, 3, etc. You can see the value of each letter below.

I = 1
V = 5
X = 10
L = 50
C = 100
D = 500
M = 1,000

If you put a smaller numeral in front of a larger numeral, such as IX, you need to subtract. So, IX is equal to 10 − 1, or 9. You can see the values of some Roman numerals below.

Examples:

IX = 9
LXI = 61
CCCXXXIII = 333
CDXLIV = 444
MXVIII = 1,018
MMVI = 2,006

The trick to understanding Roman numerals is remembering the sequence of letters. One way to do this is with an acronym about Ivy's XL Coat. Ivy sounds like I and V, the X and L are the next two values, and so on.

IT'S YOUR TURN

Write your own acronym for the Roman numeral system! Try to come up with something that will be memorable to *you*. The letter *x* is tough, so here are some ideas: *X*-rays, *x*-files, *X*-mas, or xylophone.

Rational vs. Irrational Numbers

Rational numbers are numbers that can be expressed as a fraction where the numerator and denominator are integers and the denominator does not equal 0. For example, 0.5 (which can be shown as $\frac{1}{2}$), $-\frac{9}{4}$, and 3 (which can be shown as $\frac{3}{1}$) are all rational numbers.

Irrational numbers are numbers that cannot be expressed in fraction form. For example, $\sqrt{3}$, π, and 2.1468284903 . . . are irrational numbers. In decimal form, irrational numbers go on forever and do not repeat.

▶ To remember the difference between irrational and rational numbers, imagine a crazy person (with a pie representing π!) ranting in a never-ending, never-repeating tirade.

. . . .
IT'S YOUR TURN
Write something rational. Be sure it ends with a period. (You can also repeat yourself! You can also repeat yourself!)

Hello.

Back when I was Queen of Delaware I used to think that squirrels were funny but now that I'm a purple superhero and I have more things to feed, such as my rat and my 37 cats, the most incredible animals in the universe because they can communicate with aliens much better than people who don't understand you because they're too busy worshipping street lamps and also blah, blah . . .

Rational: Ending

Irrational: Never-ending, never-repeating

The Order of Operations

▶ Please Excuse My Dear Aunt Sally.

The **order of operations** is the order that you should perform operations to simplify algebraic expressions. This famous mnemonic will help you remember the order in which to perform each operation. The first letter of each word stands for a mathematical symbol or operation.

The **P** stands for parentheses. You should always complete operations inside parentheses first. The **E** stands for exponents. You should always deal with exponents second. The **M** and **D** stand for multiplication and division. You should perform these operations in the order that they appear in the algebraic expression, from left to right. Finally, the **A** and **S** stand for addition and subtraction. Again, perform these operations in the order that they appear from left to right.

So, to simplify $3 + 2^2 \times 7 - (9 - 8) \div 0.5$, you must follow the rules of "Please Excuse My Dear Aunt Sally."

Parentheses: $3 + 2^2 \times 7 - (\mathbf{9 - 8}) \div 0.5 = 3 + 2^2 \times 7 - 1 \div 0.5$

Exponents: $3 + \mathbf{2^2} \times 7 - 1 \div 0.5 = 3 + 4 \times 7 - 1 \div 0.5$

Multiplication/Division (from left to right): $3 + \mathbf{4 \times 7} - \mathbf{1} \div \mathbf{0.5} =$
$$3 + \mathbf{28} - \mathbf{2}$$

Addition/Subtraction (from left to right): $\mathbf{3 + 28 - 2 = 29}$

The expression $3 + 2^2 \times 7 - (9 - 8) \div 0.5$ is equal to 29.

Imagine your hypothetical Aunt Sally doing something that she should be excused for. Did she sneeze? Did she belch? Maybe she did something *very* inappropriate. Invent an image for your Aunt Sally, and decide what awful thing she did.

Parts of a Fraction

► The n**U**merator is **U**p, the **D**enominator is **D**own.

Fractions represent parts of a whole or parts of a set. The number above the fraction bar is called the **numerator,** and it tells the number of parts being counted. The number below the fraction bar is called the **denominator,** and it tells the total number of equal parts. The word *numerator* has the letter *u*, which can remind you of the word *up*. The word *denominator* starts with the letter *d*, which can remind you of the word *down*.

To help remember which part of the fraction is the numerator and which is the denominator, you may want to visualize the word *numerator* above the word *denominator*. For example, remember the following image:

$$\frac{numerator}{denominator}$$

You could even write each term on a separate index card. Then, find a horizontal bar, like the towel bar in the bathroom. Tape the word *numerator* to the wall above the bar and tape the word *denominator* to the wall below the bar. This way, you'll have a visual reminder every time you dry off!

Find a map, atlas, or globe in your home. Then, find a place that starts with the letter **N**, and another place that starts with the letter **D** that is farther down (south) on the map.

For example, the **N**orth Pole is as far *up* on the globe you can go. The **D**ominican Republic is *below* the **N**orth Pole. If you can associate two places where the **N** place is over the **D** place, you'll remember the parts of the fractions forever.

Dividing Fractions

► **Keep Changing Fractions**

Dividing fractions can get complicated. You have to change something in the original problem. How can you remember what you have to do? To divide fractions, you need to *keep changing fractions*. Each first letter stands for the step you need to take, in order, to simplify a fraction by using division.

K: Keep the first fraction.
C: Change the divide sign to a multiply sign.
F: Flip the last fraction.

For example, to simplify $\frac{3}{4} \div \frac{1}{8}$ follow the steps.

K: Keep the first fraction $\frac{3}{4}$.

C: Change ÷ to ×.

F: Flip the last fraction. $\frac{3}{4} \times \frac{8}{1}$

Now you can just multiply. $\frac{3}{4} \times \frac{8}{1} = \frac{3 \times 8}{4 \times 1} = \frac{24}{4} = 6$

 Repeat the following rhyme out loud over and over until you can remember it in your sleep:

The fraction you are dividing by,
turn upside down and multiply.

Easy as Pi!

You probably don't need to memorize pi to 42,195 digits—something Hiroyuki Goto did in 1995. But it certainly helps to know the numbers for each digit up to several places. You can check your work on diameter problems, and you can solve for a circumference to a better degree of accuracy. You can also impress teachers and friends with your incredible knowledge of the irrational number pi.

To remember the digits of pi, read the sentences below. Each one contains a different number of words, and each word has the same number of letters as the value of the digit in the place of pi. You only have to know one of these sentences; it depends on how many digits of pi you want to memorize!

3. 1 4 1 5

▶ Yes, I know a digit.

3. 1 4 1 5 9

▶ Wow, I made a great discovery!

3. 1 4 1 5 9 2 6 5 3

▶ May I have a large container of orange juice now?

Get This . . .

Albert Einstein was born on March 14. That date can also be written as 3.14, or an approximation for pi. Maybe that's why Einstein was such a genius!

Decimal Places

The terms **tenths, hundredths,** and **thousandths** are the most common decimal places. Each one represents a different place value to the right of the decimal point. They represent $\frac{1}{\textbf{ten}}$, $\frac{1}{\textbf{one hundred}}$, and $\frac{1}{\textbf{one thousand}}$ respectively. To remember how many zeros are to the right of the decimal point in each decimal value, look to the number of *O*s in the text. Each letter *O* should represent a number 0 for this mnemonic.

▶ • How many times does the letter *O* appear in the number **ten**? None! That is the number of zeros to the right of the decimal point in a **tenth**.

• How many times does the letter *O* appear in the number **one hundred**? One! That is the number of zeros to the right of the decimal point in one **hundredth**.

• How many times does the letter *O* appear in the number **one thousand**? Two! That is the number of zeros to the right of the decimal point in one **thousandth**.

Tenth = 0.1

One Hundredth = 0.**0**1

One Th**O**sandth = 0.**00**1

Draw arrows from the *O*s in bold above to the 0s to the right of the decimal point. If this is your book, go ahead and write on the page. If it's from your school or library (or a friend), write out the examples on a separate piece of paper.

Mean, Median, and Mode

▶ Someone who calls you **average** is being **mean**.
The **median** of the highway is in the **middle**.
The **mode** is the number that appears **most** often.

You can learn about a list of numbers by finding its mean, median, or mode. These terms give you information about the values, and it's super important that you don't mix them up. To avoid confusion, simply create associations with the terms, such as above.

The **mean** is the **average** value of a set of numbers. To find the mean, add all the values together, and then divide the sum by the number of values.

The **median** is the **middle** value in a set of numbers. To find the median, put the numbers in order, and find the value in the middle. If there is an even number of values in the set, average the two middle numbers.

The **mode** is the number that occurs the **most often** in a set of numbers. (Both terms begin with *mo.*) There can be no mode—or more than one mode—in a set of numbers.

For example, look at the following values:
   20, 52, 26, 24, 18, 20, 23, 16, 25

The **mean** is the average. Add all the values together and divide by the number of terms.
   $20 + 52 + 26 + 24 + 18 + 20 + 23 + 16 + 25 = 224 \div 8 = 28$

The **median** is the middle number. First, put the values in order, and then find the value in the middle.
   16, 18, 20, 20, (23), 24, 25, 26, 52

The **mode** is the value that occurs most often:
   16, 18, (20, 20), 23, 24, 25, 26, 52

Imagine that someone you know calls you **average** at something you think you do well. Would you get **mean**? Act out your response to being called average!

The Properties of Properties

You'll use the following properties throughout your life with math.

The **commutative property of addition** states that $a + b = b + a$.
The **commutative property of multiplication** states that $ab = ba$.

The **associative property of addition** states that $(a + b) + c = a + (b + c)$.
The **associative property of multiplication** states that $(ab)c = a(bc)$.

The **distributive property** states that $a(b + c) = ab + ac$.
To remember each property, make the following connections.

▶ When you **commute** from home to school, the distance is the same in each direction. For example, let's say you have to walk to the bus stop and take the bus to school. That's the same distance as taking the bus from school to the bus stop, then walking home. That's like the commutative property.

▶ If you **associate** with a group of friends, it means you are connected together. For example, let's say your name is Adam and your two best friends are Barry and Chris. It doesn't matter if two of you are grouped at one time, you're still the same group of friends! This is like the **associative property**, where the grouping does not change the values.

▶ If your math teacher **distributes** a pop quiz to your class, that means he or she makes a copy and gives it to everyone. The **distributive property** essentially "gives" the value outside the parentheses to all the values inside it.

Do a nice deed, and **distribute** a few small gifts to your friends and family. You'll have to give the same number of gifts to everyone, or else it wouldn't be fair. For example, if you have 16 people to give your gifts to—7 friends and 9 family members—and you want to give them each 3 marbles, that's the same as giving 3 marbles to 7 friends and 9 family members individually. The distributive property shows that $3(7 + 9)$ and $3(7) + 3(9)$ are equal.

Scientific Notation

▶ **Positive** power, move in the **positive** direction
Negative power, move in the **negative** direction

Scientific notation is a way to represent very large numbers and very small numbers. All scientific notation is written in the form $N \times 10\#$, where N is a number greater than or equal to 1 and smaller than 10. There can only be a single digit before the decimal point, and the power of ten tells you how many places and in which direction to move the decimal point.

Look at examples of places of scientific notation with a positive exponent and a negative exponent.

4.2×10^7 has a power of 7, which is positive. So this must be a large number. Count the 7 places to the right of the decimal point. (That makes the number bigger!)

$$4.2 \times 10^{7} = 4.2000000.$$
+1 +2 +3 +4 +5 +6 +7

9.06×10^{-4} has a power of −4, which is negative. So this must be a small number. Count the 4 places to the left of the decimal point. (That makes the number smaller!)

$$9.06 \times 10^{-4} = .0009.06$$
−4 −3 −2 −1

. . . .
IT'S YOUR TURN

Determine the scientific notation for a number you use in your daily life. How many seconds are there in an hour? How many kilometers long is your foot? How old is your mom or dad? (Show your parent their age in scientific notation; they'll appreciate it.)

Theoretical and Experimental Probability

▶ Theoretical probability is what you **th**ink will happen.
Experimental probability is what you **exp**erience happening.

Theoretical probability is a ratio of the number of ways that an event can occur to the total number of possibilities. You can determine theoretical probability with the following ratio:

$$\frac{\text{the number of ways an event can occur}}{\text{the total number of possibilities}}$$

If you flipped a quarter, the theoretical probability that it will land on heads is $\frac{1}{2}$, because there is one way the event can occur and two total possibilities.

Experimental probability is a ratio of the number of times an event occurred to the number of total times that it was attempted. You can determine experimental probability with the following ratio:

$$\frac{\text{the number of ways an event occurred}}{\text{the total number of attempts}}$$

If you flipped that same quarter 10 times, and it ended up on heads 7 times, the experimental probability that it will land on heads is $\frac{7}{10}$. That is because the event occurred 7 times, and there were 10 attempts. (A greater number of attempts usually results in greater accuracy of probability!)

IT'S YOUR TURN

Break out a deck of cards or a six-sided die. Consider what you think the theoretical probability will be of picking an ace, or rolling a 6. Then, try your own experiment. Pick 13 cards (each time replacing the card you picked), or roll the die six times. How did the experimental probability match up with your theoretical probability?

Multiplying binomials

► FOIL

A **binomial** is a polynomial with two terms. When you multiply two binomials such as $(x + 2)(x + 3)$, each term in the first binomial must be multiplied by each term in the second binomial. To do this in a systematic way, use the FOIL method.

First: Multiply together the first terms in each binomial: $x \bullet x = x^2$.

Outside: Multiply the first term of the first binomial by the second term in the second binomial: $x \bullet 3 = 3x$.

Inside: Multiply the second term of the first binomial by the first term of the second binomial: $2 \bullet x = 2x$.

Last: Multiply together the last terms of each binomial: $2 \bullet 3 = 6$.

After you have multiplied the terms, be sure to simplify and combine like terms: $x^2 + 2x + 3x + 6 = x^2 + 5x + 6$.

You may find it useful to draw a line to connect the terms that are supposed to be multiplied. As you connect the first terms in each binomial, write "first" above the line. Continue until you have connected the outside, inside, and last terms. By connecting the terms of the binomials, you can check that each term in the first binomial is indeed multiplied by each term in the second binomial.

Reducing Radicals

When you work with radicals, you need to reduce the number inside the radical as much as possible. Sometimes an index with the radical tells you how many times a factor can be factored out of the radical. Look at the example below.

▶ To remember and understand how to simplify a radical with an index, think of the radical as a jail and the index as bail. You need to make bail to get out of jail!

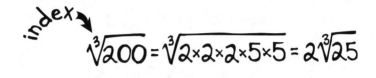

$$\sqrt[3]{200} = \sqrt[3]{2 \times 2 \times 2 \times 5 \times 5} = 2\sqrt[3]{25}$$

In the example above, the bail is 3. There are three 2s, so they can make bail—and get out of jail. There are only two 5s, so they don't make bail—they stay in jail. That's why $5 \times 5 = 25$ remains in the radical; the 5s can't come out. The answer is $2\sqrt[3]{25}$.

Another example is $\sqrt[4]{162}$. Because this is equivalent to $\sqrt[4]{3 \times 3 \times 3 \times 3 \times 2}$, you can get the 3s out of jail! (It meets the index/bail of 4!) The answer is $3\sqrt[4]{2}$.

Draw bar cells around the radical to illustrate the "stuck in jail" notion of this mnemonic. Remember that for a factor to get out of jail, you need as many as the index tells you.

Inverse Variation

▶ Inverse Variation = Invert Variable

There are many different ways in which variables can relate to each other. An **inverse variation** between x and y is one where as x increases, y decreases. This relationship can also be stated as: y varies *inversely* with x. An equation to represent this is $y = \dfrac{k}{x}$, where k is called the constant of variation. To remember the equation for an inverse variation, use the mnemonic above. *Invert variable* will help you remember that x, the variable, is *inverted*, or is in the denominator.

An example of inverse variation is the relationship between the length and width of a rectangle given a certain area. Suppose the area of a rectangle is 24 square units. Let x represent the length and y represent the width. Then, we know that $xy = 24$, or $y = \dfrac{24}{x}$. The constant of variation, k, in this example is 24. Notice that as the value of x, the length, increases, the value of y, the width, decreases.

Using a ruler, draw a rectangle with area 24 square centimeters. Start with the lengths of the sides as: length = 1 centimeter, and width = 24 centimeters. Keep drawing different rectangles of the same area, and let the value of the length increase. Use the formula to help you figure out the value of the width as the length increases. Continue to draw the rectangles for increasing values of x.

Notice how the increasing value of the length causes a decreasing value of the width. How large do you think you could let the length get? Is there a smallest possible value for the width?

The Quadratic Formula

You can use the **quadratic formula** to solve quadratic equations for the coefficients a, b, and c. For the formula to work, a cannot be zero. (You can't have zero in the denominator of a fraction, ever!)

The formula is given below.

$$x = \frac{-b \pm \sqrt{b^2 - 4ac}}{2a}$$

The solutions of the quadratic formula are the roots of the equation.

However complicated the quadratic formula might appear, you simply need to know it. It's not the most memorable formula, of course, so it may help to give it a rhyme or rhythm. Sing the following lines to the old nursery rhyme "Pop Goes the Weasel."

Sung to the tune of "Pop Goes the Weasel":
> x equals negative b
> Plus or minus square root
> of b squared minus four a c
> All over two a.

This mnemonic won't help you at all unless you sing it out loud to the tune of the song. If you don't know how "Pop Goes the Weasel" is sung, ask a friend or a parent. Once you get it, repeat it over and over until it becomes one of those really annoying songs that you can't get out of your head. (It may be irritating, but you'll ace your math tests as a result!)

Parallel vs. Perpendicular

Parallel lines are lines in a plane that never meet or intersect.

Perpendicular lines are lines that form right (90-degree) angles.

▶ To remember which is which, notice the parallel lines in the word *parallel.*

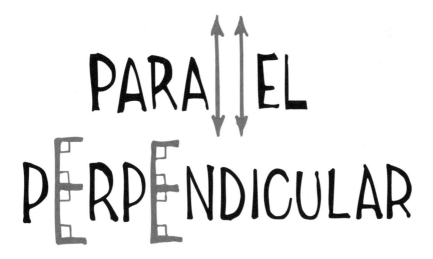

Remember that a right angle is often written with a small square in the corner of the angle. The letter E has 3 perpendicular lines, making 4 right angles. So, you might also notice that the word *perpendicular* has more perpendicular lines than parallel.

Draw two vertical parallel lines on a sheet of graph paper. Then, write the letters "P A R A" to the left of your lines. Then, write the letters "E L" to the right of your lines. Do you see what you've drawn?

Angle Types

There are three basic types of angles: acute, right, and obtuse.

An **acute** angle has a measure of less than 90 degrees.
A **right** angle has a measure of exactly 90 degrees.
An **obtuse** angle has a measure of more than 90 degrees.

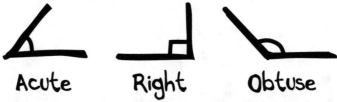

Acute   Right   Obtuse

A right triangle has two sides that are perpendicular, which means they meet at a 90-degree angle. The back and seat of a chair also meet at a right angle. Imagining a person sitting up straight—the "right" way—in a chair will help you remember the definition of a right angle.

▶ The **right** way to sit is to form a 90-degree angle in your chair.

The two sides that meet at right angles are called the *legs* of the triangle. The side opposite the right angle is called the *hypotenuse*. (See page 166 for a great mnemonic for the hypotenuse!)

▶ **A cute** puppy is a small dog. An acute angle is a small angle.

a cute puppy

acute angle

▶ An **obese** dog is a very large dog. An obtuse angle is a large angle.

obese dog

obtuse angle

A "cute" puppy or kitten is a lot smaller than a full-grown dog or cat. So an acute angle is a small angle. If you associate the word *obtuse* with *obese*, you'll never forget which is a big angle!

Sit up straight in your chair! Make sure your legs are perfectly perpendicular to your back. Repeat to yourself, "I am sitting the *right* way. I am sitting the *right* way."

The Hypotenuse

The **hypotenuse** is the longest side of any right triangle. It's the side directly across from the right angle. (It almost looks like the right angle "points" to the hypotenuse.) No matter what the measures of the legs are, the hypotenuse will always be the longest.

Look at the triangle below. What do you notice about the sides and their respective names?

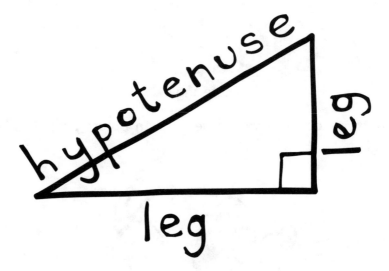

The word *leg* is really short. The word *hypotenuse* is really long. Just by looking at the names of each side, you can tell which side will be the longest.

► *Hypotenuse* is a long word to spell, and it's the longest part of a right triangle!

Say the words *leg, leg* really quickly—as quickly as you can. Say the word *hy-pot-e-nuse* really slowly, drawing out each syllable. This will help you recall that the hypotenuse is the longest part of a right triangle, and the legs are the shorter sides.

The Axis of Y

It is very, very, very important that you know which axis on a coordinate plane is the *x*-axis and which one is the *y*-axis. To remember which is which, take a look at the capital letter *Y*.

Do you see the vertical line at the bottom of the **Y**? That is because the *y*-axis is the *vertical* axis! Place it right on the coordinate grid, and you'll see how it fits.

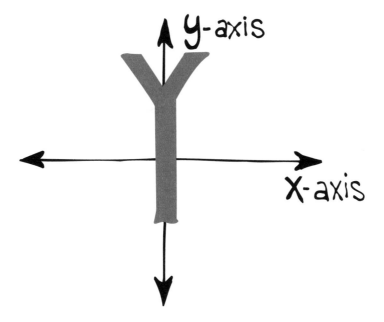

 So you've seen which is the *y*-axis. Just so you're sure, draw Xs all over the *x*-axis. X marks the spot, right?

Order of the Coordinate Pair

It's a common error to confuse the order of the *x*- and *y*-coordinates in a coordinate pair. To help remember which one comes first, just remember the following rhyme.

▶ *x* before *y*, **walk** before you **fly**.

Look at the coordinate grid on the following page. Check out the guy walking across the *x*-axis, then flying up alongside the *y*-axis.

Let's see how to find the location of (6, 10). Remember, first **walk.** The guy can walk left or right. According to the coordinate pair (6, 10), the guy needs to walk 6 spaces to the right—or to the point (6, 0). Next, the guy can fly up or down. According to the coordinate pair (6, 10), the guy needs to fly 10 spaces up. Now, he's at (6, 10). He is 10 spaces above the origin. And he's 6 spaces to the right of the origin.

So, all you have to do is realize that the first number in the coordinate pair means where to **walk.** In this case, that is 6 points to the right of the origin. Then, you get to **fly!** And here, that's all the way up 10 points to (6, 10).

You can remember this mnemonic any time you have to locate the placement of an ordered pair on a coordinate grid. How far (and in which direction) do you have to walk? Then, how far (and in which direction) do you have to fly?

(6,10)

Say the alphabet out loud. When you get to the end, slow down and pronounce *x* and *y* carefully. Notice how *x* comes before *y*? *Exactly!*

Quadrants of the Coordinate Plane

The first quadrant on the coordinate plane is in the upper right-hand corner, and then the next three quadrants follow in counterclockwise order. But it's not always easy to remember which quadrant is which.

▶ All you have to do is write a "**C**" for "**C**oordinate Grid" *on* the grid, and you'll know the correct order of the quadrants!

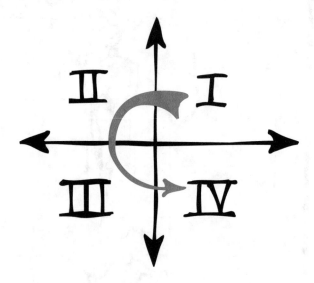

Draw your own coordinate grid, labeling both the *x*- and *y*-axes. Then, write a giant *C* on the grid, making sure that the *C* starts in the top-right quadrant and ends in the bottom-right quadrant. Finally, label each quadrant I–IV according to the direction you drew your giant *C*!

Rays

A **ray** is an important geometric term. It is part of a straight line that extends forever in one direction only. A *line* continues forever in both directions, and a *line segment* has both a starting and an ending point. In contrast, a *ray* has only a starting point and no endpoint. (For a ray to be a ray, it needs an arrow on one end and a point on the other.)

▶ To avoid confusing the different line terms, think about rays of sunlight extending forever from the sun. That's a **ray of sunlight**.

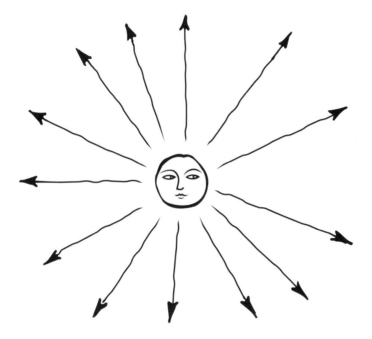

 Make a drawing that shows the expression "Catch some rays." Be sure to include actual rays in your picture.

Scalene – Isosceles – Equilateral

There are many ways to classify a triangle. One way is to count the number of congruent sides. (Congruent sides are sides of equal measure.)

• A triangle with three congruent sides is called **equilateral.**

• A triangle with two congruent sides is called **isosceles.**

• A triangle with no congruent sides is **scalene.**

► To remember which word means which, look at the first letter of each term: E, I, and S.

- There are **3 congruent**, horizontal lines in the letter **E**. That is the number of congruent sides in an equilateral triangle.
- There are **2 congruent**, horizontal lines in the letter **I**. That is the minimum number of congruent sides in an isosceles triangle.
- There are **no congruent**, horizontal lines in the letter **S**. That is the number of congruent sides in a scalene triangle.

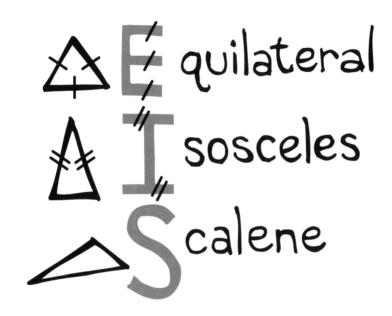

Draw your own equilateral, isosceles, and scalene triangles. Use a ruler to make sure you draw 3, 2, and no congruent sides for the three triangles.

Properties of an Isosceles Triangle

Isosceles triangles have two sides of equal length and two angles of equal measure. To help recall their attributes, read the ridiculous song to the tune of "Oh Christmas Tree!" (If you don't know it, come up with your own melody.)

▶ Oh isosceles, oh isosceles...
Two angles have
equal degrees.

Oh isosceles, oh isosceles...
Two sides alike
just like my knees.

Oh isosceles, oh isosceles...
You look just like
a Christmas tree.

 Look around your home for isosceles triangles. You can find them everywhere—in a flag, the roof of a house, or in a bag of tortilla chips.

Complementary vs. Supplementary Angles

Complementary angles are angles whose measures add up to 90 degrees. **Supplementary angles** are angles whose measures add up to 180 degrees.

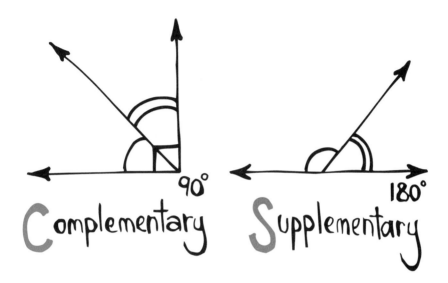

It's easy to confuse these important mathematical terms. And any time you're tested on this vocabulary, you'll have to know which is which. So how can you tell them apart?

▶ First of all, the terms are in order: *Complementary* angles come before *supplementary* angles, both in terms of the measure of their angles and their order in the dictionary.

But for a sure-fire way to remember, look at the first letter of each term: *C* and *S*. The *S* is made up of two *C*s (one is backward). That shows that the *S* is double the *C*—just as the measure of supplementary angles is twice that of the measure of complementary angles!

Open up a dictionary to the word *complementary*. Then, flip to the word *supplementary* in the dictionary. Did you notice how the word *complementary* comes first?

The Slope of a Line

When you work with lines on a coordinate grid, undoubtedly you'll be dealing with their slopes. The **slope of a line** is the *steepness* of the line. Questions on tests will often ask you to find the slope of a line, use a slope to find points on a line, or use slope to find parallel or perpendicular lines. You can determine the slope of a line by plugging points into the formula $m = \dfrac{y_2 - y_1}{x_2 - x_1}$ where m = slope and $x_2 - x_1 \neq 0$.

If you can tell whether a slope is positive, negative, zero, or undefined, you'll be in great shape. You'll be able to check your answer or get rid of wrong answer choices on a multiple-choice test. To do this, imagine that the line is a hill and you are walking on the line.

▶ Going from left to right, how would you walk up the hill? Up. That's a **positive slope**.

▶ Going from right to left, how would you walk down the hill? Down. That's a **negative slope**.

▶ Going from left to right, how would you walk if it's flat? There is no hill! So there is **zero slope**.

▶ What if you *can't* walk on the hill from left to right? Then what? It must be **undefined**.

Take a look at pictures of downhill skiers or snowboarders. (Look on the Internet, or find a picture in a sports magazine.) They go down negative slopes. How fast would they be going if the slope was zero? Probably about 0 mph. How about if the slope were undefined?

Positive and Negative Parabolas

When you graph the equation of a line on a coordinate grid, you get a straight line. When an equation contains an exponent of 2, its graph is a parabola. That's a curved shape that looks like the letter U.

Equations for parabolas are in the standard form $y = \boldsymbol{a}x^2 + \boldsymbol{b}x + \boldsymbol{c}$. The a part of the equation tells you whether the parabola is positive or negative. If it's positive, the parabola opens up and looks like a smile. If a is negative, the parabola opens down and looks like a frown.

You may not always see all parts of the standard form. For example, if the equation is $y = 1x^2 + 0x + 1$, you would only see it as $y = x^2 + 1$. (The coefficient 1 is implied.)

For example, the two parabolas on the following page are $y = x^2 + 1$ and $y = -x^2 - 1$. You can determine their points by plugging in values for x and finding the corresponding values for y. See below.

► To remember the difference between positive and negative parabolas, just look at their shapes. The one that looks like a smile is positive. The one that looks like a frown is negative. The eyes drawn above the parabolas show that they're like faces. The positive parabola looks positive, and the negative parabola looks, well, negative!

$$y = x^2 + 1$$

x	y
0	1
1	2
2	5
3	10

$$y = -x^2 - 1$$

x	y
0	-1
1	-2
2	-5
3	-10

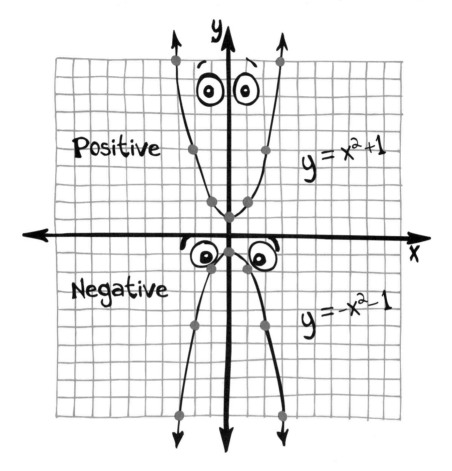

Positive

$y = x^2 + 1$

Negative

$y = -x^2 - 1$

👁 Write something positive for the positive parabola, and write something negative for the one that looks like a frown. Even writing something as silly as "I hate being a parabola" for the negative parabola will help you remember the difference!

Transformations

Reflection, translation, and rotation are three of the most common geometric transformations. They can turn a triangle upside-down, reflect a rhombus, or shift an octagon to anywhere on the coordinate grid. (Congruent images have corresponding sides that have the same lengths and corresponding angles that have the same measures.)

Reflection is a transformation that produces a congruent image *reflected* over a line. The line is called a *reflection line*, which can be the *x*- or *y*-axis.

Rotation is a transformation that produces a congruent image *rotated* around a point.

Slide is a transformation that produces a congruent image where each point of the image is moved the same distance. A slide is also called a **translation.**

See the three transformations on the coordinate grid below.

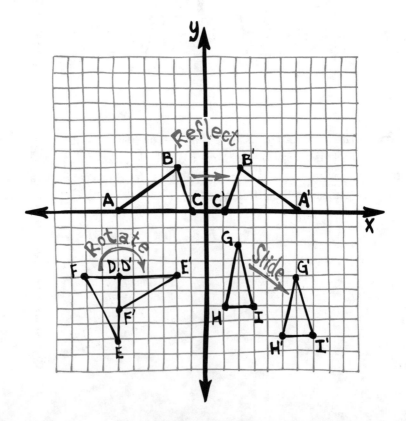

How to Remember Everything • Grades 9-12

One trick for remembering each transformation is to recognize the root word for each transformation. Create an image of each, and you'll never mix up the transformations again! See the following pages.

▶ When you're considering a **reflection**, think about a reflection in a mirror. What happens when you raise your right hand in a mirror? Imagine that you're holding a polygon. What would happen to the polygon? The same thing happens to a polygon reflected in a coordinate grid.

Reflection

▶ Have you ever gone on a **slide** before? When you ride on a slide, you go from the top to the bottom, and you usually move horizontally too. And when you get to the end, are you the same person? Do you have the same shape? Of course! The same rule applies to a slide on a coordinate grid—a figure is shifted, but it doesn't change orientation, shape, or size. (Just keep in mind that a slide on a coordinate grid is not tied to gravity—so it can go in any direction!)

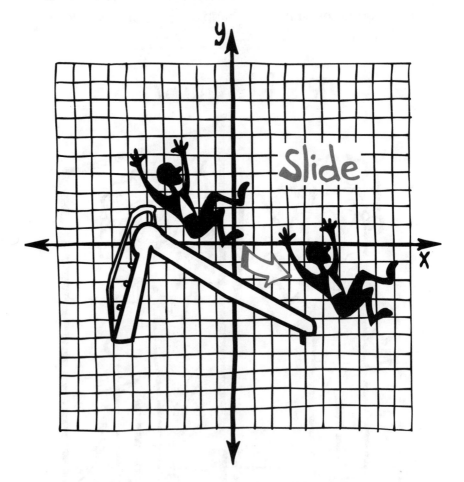

▶ **Rotation** is the noun form of *rotate*. What do you think of when you hear the verb *rotate*? A tire might rotate on a bike or a car. And what happens to it as it rotates? It stays the same, essentially; it just gets turned around. It can be turned a few degrees, or it can be completely upside down. If it gets rotated *all the way around*, well, then it looks exactly the same.

Draw a polygon on a piece of paper. Then, fold the paper any way you want, as long as the crease doesn't go over your figure. Then, draw a shape on the other side of the crease so that the new figure matches up with the polygon you originally drew. (When you fold the paper, the two drawings should match up perfectly.) When you're done, you'll have created a reflection—using the crease in the paper as your reflection line!

Area and Circumference of a Circle

▶ For a circle,
apple pies are square.
Cherry pies are too!

Most apple pies aren't really square, but maybe a circle would feel strange about eating pies that were shaped like itself! This chaining mnemonic will help you remember the formulas for the area and the circumference of a circle!

The **area** of a circle is the amount of space inside the circle. The second line of the mnemonic represents the formula for the area of a circle: $A = \pi r^2$. *Apple* stands for *A*, or area. *Pies* stands for the number π. And *are square* represents r^2, the radius of the circle being squared.

The **circumference** of a circle is the distance around the circle. The third line of the mnemonic represents the formula for the circumference of a circle: $C = 2\pi r$. *Cherry* stands for *C*, or circumference. Again, *pies* stand for the number π. Finally, *are too* represents *r*, the radius, times 2. Notice that the order of the multiplication is different. Our mnemonic actually stands for $C = \pi r \cdot 2$. But multiplication is commutative, so the order doesn't matter!

In this case, remembering the picture will aid you in remembering the mnemonic. It's important to picture the circle holding the two types of square pies because it will help you remember that these two formulas apply to a circle. But be careful! It is important to remember which formula applies to which type of pie! If you simply memorize the picture, it may be difficult to remember how the picture relates to the formulas. So use the picture, but also say the mnemonic over and over in your head until you've memorized it. And if you forget which type of pie comes first in the mnemonic, just remember that *apple* comes before *cherry* alphabetically.

Pythagorean Theorem

▶ I saw a square hippo with two square legs!

The **Pythagorean theorem** states that the square of the length of the hypotenuse is equal to the sum of the squares of the lengths of the two other sides: $c^2 = a^2 + b^2$ where c equals the length of the hypotenuse.

The *square hippo* in this mnemonic will help you remember to square the hypotenuse (c^2). The word *with* can help you remember that there should be an equal sign. The *two square legs* mean that you should square the length of each leg of the triangle and then add them together ($a^2 + b^2$). When you think of the Pythagorean theorem, you can think of this silly picture of a square hippo with two square legs. You can even name the hippo Pythagoras, the Greek mathematician who discovered this theorem!

Here is an example of the Pythagorean theorem.

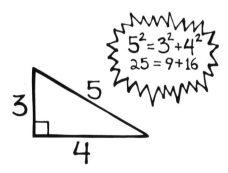

It's Your Turn

Chaining is a useful mnemonic tool to help you remember formulas. You should use words and phrases that have special meaning for you. For example, if it is difficult for you to remember where the equal sign goes in the Pythagorean theorem, you can come up with a word that will always mean "equal" to you. The Pythagorean theorem is also written as $a^2 + b^2 = c^2$, where a and b represent the legs of the triangle and c represents the hypotenuse. See if you can come up with a chaining mnemonic to remember $a^2 + b^2 = c^2$. To represent the variables, you might want to use words that start with the letters a, b, and c. You can even pick words that you'll always use to represent those variables.

Cups, Pints, and Quarts

Say you're in a friend's kitchen, whipping up a batch of brownies for a bake sale. The recipe calls for a cup of flour, but none of your friend's measuring cups are labeled. What do you do? (You can't go to the store, that's cheating.)

It may help to remember the correct order of cups, pints, and quarts. One helpful way is to recognize the lengths of the words. A **cup** is smaller than a **pint.** A pint is smaller than a **quart.**

A **cup** is half a **pint,** which is half a **quart.** (And a *quart,* of course, is a *quarter* of a gallon!)

 Draw the words *cup, pint,* and *quart* on a piece of paper. Try to space it out so that 2 cups equals 1 pint, or 4 cups equals 1 quart!

The Metric Units of Measurement

▶ King Henry Died By Drinking Chocolate Milk.

Kilo–
Hecto–
Deka–
Base
Deci–
Centi–
Milli–

The metric units of measurement are used from everything from beverages (liters) to computer storage systems (megabytes). Once you get the hang of it, the metric system is actually easier than our English system because it is based on powers of 10.

Kilo– means 1,000 times the base number. **Hecto–** means 100 times the base number. **Deka–** means 10 times the base number. **Deci–** means one-tenth times the base number. **Centi–** means one-hundredth times the base number. **Milli–** means one-thousandth times the base number.

You can find these roots in the English language. How many years are in a decade? A century? A millennium? Have you ever seen a centipede? How about a millipede? (Okay, maybe they don't have 1,000 legs—but it sure seems like it!)

Sit like a king in your chair in a very stately manner. Bring one liter of chocolate milk to your lips. As you drink, pretend to start to choke and fall off your chair! Remember that that is how King Henry died, at least according to the mnemonic. (Be sure to clean up any spilled chocolate milk that may result from this activity.)

❝*Get This . . .*
When the real King Henry died (not from drinking chocolate milk), his body was buried in one place, while his eyes, brain, and entrails were buried somewhere else! **❞**

SOH-CAH-TOA

If you know one side of a right triangle and the measure of an angle (besides the right angle), you can determine the lengths of the other two sides using the trigonometric ratios. For example, look at the triangle below, showing an angle marked A.

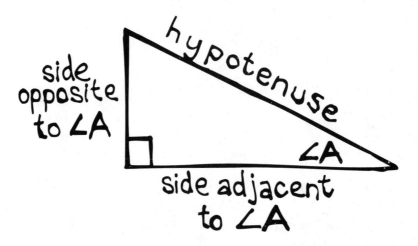

If you know the measure of ∠A and the length of the hypotenuse, you can calculate the lengths of the opposite and adjacent sides. You just have to use the three trigonometric formulas shown below:

$$\text{sine } A = \frac{\text{side opposite } \angle A}{\text{hypotenuse}}$$

$$\text{cosine } A = \frac{\text{side adjacent } \angle A}{\text{hypotenuse}}$$

$$\text{tangent } A = \frac{\text{side opposite } \angle A}{\text{side adjacent } \angle A}$$

Suppose ∠A measures 50 degrees, the hypotenuse is 14 cm, and you want to find the length of the opposite side. You will use the sine ratio.

$$\text{sine } 50° = \frac{\text{side opposite } \angle A}{14 \text{ cm}}$$

Multiply each side of the equation by 14 so that 14 × sine 50° = side opposite ∠A.

Then, use your calculator to find that sine 50° = 0.76604, which when multiplied by 14, gives 10.7246 cm. That's the length of the side opposite ∠A.

You can also use these trigonometric functions to find the measure of the angle.

You just need to know the lengths of two sides.

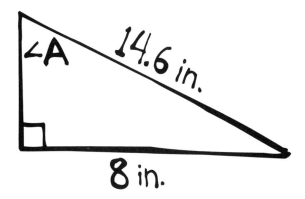

Plugging in the lengths according to the function, you will get sine $A = \dfrac{8}{14.6}$. That is equal to sine $A = 0.5479$. From there, use the inverse sin button on the calculator, and you will find that $A = 33°$.

These trigonometric ratios are *very* important, and you will use them often. Millions of students across the country have used a famous mnemonic to remember them:

▶ SOH-CAH-TOA

It is pronounced "so-kah-toe-ah." It sounds like it could be a Native American word, though it really doesn't mean anything. It's an acronym for the three functions:

The SOH stands for "**S**ine of an angle is **O**pposite over **H**ypotenuse."

The CAH stands for "**C**osine of an angle is **A**djacent over **H**ypotenuse."

The TOA stands for "**T**angent of an angle is **O**pposite over **A**djacent."

Trigonometric Ratios

A different trigonometric ratio is positive for each quadrant of the coordinate grid. See below for a breakdown of the four quadrants.

In quadrant I, **A**ll trigonometric ratios are positive.

In quadrant II, **S**ine ratios are positive.

In quadrant III, **T**angent ratios are positive.

In quadrant IV, **C**osine ratios are positive.

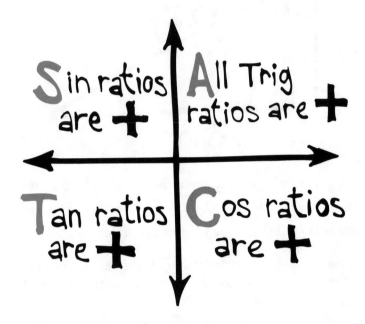

To remember which quadrants are positive for which trigonometric ratios, use the following acrostic:

▶ **A**ll **S**tudents **T**ake **C**alculus.

The letters **A**, **S**, **T**, and **C** remind us which quadrant is positive, going in counterclockwise order around the quadrants. (You can use the mnemonic on page 170 to recall which quadrant is which.)

IT'S YOUR TURN

"All Students Take Calculus" is a nice way to remember the positive quadrants on a coordinate grid. But any four-word acrostic that has the letters A, S, T, and C (in order) will work. Come up with your own that might be more memorable to you!

Your toes can teach you mitosis!

Structural Organization

There are five increasingly complex structural levels of organization in organisms: cells, tissues, organs, organ systems, and organisms. You can use the pegword mnemonic to help you remember the order of the organism's organization.

▶ The first level is the **cell.** *One* rhymes with *bun*. To remember this first level of an organism's organization, imagine a bun in a jail cell.

The second level is **tissues.** *Two* rhymes with *shoe*. To remember this second level of an organism's organization, picture some toilet paper stuck to a shoe.

The third level is the **organ level.** *Three* rhymes with *tree*. To remember this third level of an organism's organization, imagine a tree playing an organ. The organ in the picture is musical, but it can still help you remember the body's organs.

The fourth level is the **organ systems.** *Four* rhymes with *door*. To remember this fourth level of an organism's organization, imagine a person opening a door to his digestive system. The digestive system is one organ system in the body.

The fifth level is the **organism.** *Five* rhymes with *hive*. To remember this fifth level of an organism's organization, imagine a series of bees flying out of a hive. Each bee in the picture is an organism.

. . . .
It's Your Turn

Can you think of other pictures that show the correct order of the structural elements of an organism using the pegword method? Write out a different way to remember the levels of organization in an organism, using pegwords. Remember that there are alternate meanings for the word *organ*.

Composition of the Human Body

Only six different elements make up most of (99 percent of) the human body. In terms of mass, the six elements are (in order) oxygen (O), carbon (C), hydrogen (H), nitrogen (N), calcium (Ca), and phosphorus (P). You can remember this order with the following acrostic.

▶ **O**h, **C**omposition of **H**umans **N**ow— **C**urrent **P**eople

oxygen   carbon   hydrogen   nitrogen   calcium   phosphorous

In addition to those six elements, the other common elements found in the human body include potassium (K), sulfur (S), sodium (Na), chlorine (Cl), magnesium (Mg), iodine (I), iron (Fe), and trace amounts of several other elements. You can remember the major 13 elements of the human body with the following mnemonic.

▶ See Hopkins Café, mighty good salt

C = carbon
H O P K I N S = hydrogen, oxygen, phosphorus, potassium, iodine, nitrogen, sulfur
Ca Fe = calcium, iron
Mg = magnesium
Na Cl = sodium, chlorine

To remember this mnemonic, you need to know that NaCl is the chemical compound for salt. You also need to read "See" as the letter *C*.

Write out the complete "Hopkins Café" mnemonic on a piece of paper. Then, using a pen or pencil, connect the letters and words with their corresponding elements. Use a periodic table to confirm the abbreviations.

Diploid vs. Haploid

▶ To remember whether haploid or diploid cells have one or two sets of chromosomes, just imagine the letter *i* representing a set of chromosomes. The word with one *i* has one set of chromosomes. The word with two sets of *i*'s has two sets of chromosomes. The words *haploid* and *diploid* are biological terms that tell you the number of chromosomes in a cell.

A **haploid** cell has one set of each chromosome. Fungus is usually a haploid organism. Gametes (sperm and egg cells) are haploid. Haploid cells are also occasionally referred to as monoploid cells.

A **diploid** cell has two sets of each chromosome. Most animal cells are diploid.

Look at the words *haploid* and *diploid*. Is there something about the words that would help you remember what they mean? Maybe that *haploid* sounds like "half-loid."

Mitosis

▶ **My Toes Is** divided into two identical feet.

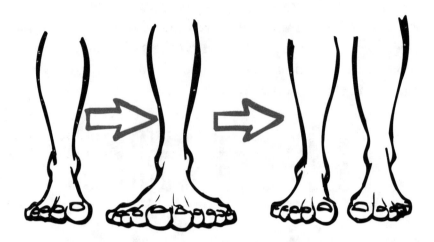

There are two basic types of cell division: meiosis and mitosis. **Mitosis,** the more common type of cell division, creates two daughter cells from a single parent cell. The daughter cells are identical to the parent. (Meiosis is cell division that results in sex cells.)

Mitosis sounds like "My Toes Is." To remember the meaning of the important biological term, consider a foot with five toes. It splits into two identical "daughter" feet with five toes each. If each foot is a cell, your *toes is* mitosis!

Stand barefoot with one foot on the ground. Then, put your feet close together, so they look like one ten-toed foot. Slowly move them apart, wiggling your toes as you go. One foot has become two identical feet. You've now acted out mitosis.

The Cell Cycle

▶ Interesting
Programs
Messed
Up
Anna's
Television.

The **cell cycle** is the life cycle of a cell. It includes the steps of cell division called mitosis (see the previous page for a visual definition!). In all, the cell cycle includes five major stages: interphase, prophase, metaphase, anaphase, and telophase.

During **interphase** the cell grows and prepares to divide. Because this stage of the cell cycle does not involve actual division, it is not technically part of mitosis.

Prophase is the first stage of mitosis. Structures called centrioles start moving to the opposite ends of the cell. Spindle fibers begin to stretch between the opposite ends of the cell.

When **metaphase** occurs, the cell begins to organize for division. Its double-stranded chromosomes align along the center of the cell. The chromosomes also attach to spindle fibers.

During **anaphase,** the strands of the chromosomes separate. Then, the strands move to opposite ends of the cell.

Telophase is the final stage of the cell cycle. Membranes develop around the nuclei of the soon-to-be daughter cells. The cell is then ready for cytokinesis, which divides the cell membrane and cytoplasm. (Cytokinesis follows the cell cycle.)

To remember the order of these five stages, you can use an acrostic with words that give clues for the names of each stage.

Picture a television with something interesting playing on the screen. Can you think of a way to make the television belong to Anna and a way that the screen might be "messed up"?

IT'S YOUR TURN

Make your own chaining story, combining elements of the five major stages of the cell cycle. For example, you can create a story of an *interesting* professional athlete who *met a* girl named *Ana* over the *tele*phone. (Or maybe Ana was so excited that she called home on the telephone—before riding home on her *cycle!*)

Cell Theory

In 1839, two German biologists, **Theodore Schwann** and **Matthias Schleiden,** published the original cell theory, which stated that all organisms are built upon a foundation of cells. This doctrine is now the basis for modern biology. The three basic conclusions from that original publication were as follows:

1. The cell is the basic unit of structure and organization in all living things.
2. The cell is at the same time both independent and a part of the organism—no matter how large or small the organism.
3. Each cell is formed by spontaneous generation.

The third statement of the original theory was flawed, however. It was disproved within a few years. In 1855, another German biologist, Rudolph Virchow, stated that "all cells come from cells." This altered the third conclusion of the cell theory to the following:

3. All cells come from cells that already exist. A cell divides to form two identical cells.

▶ To remember these three components of the cell theory, use the pegword method.

1. *One* rhymes with *bun*. To remember the first part of the cell theory (which says that all organisms are made up of cells), picture different organisms made up of hamburger buns.
2. *Two* rhymes with *shoe*. To remember the second part of the cell theory (which says that cells are both independent and part of the whole), picture shoes that are both microscopic and large.
3. *Three* rhymes with *tree*. To remember the third part of the cell theory (which says that cells are formed by other cells splitting), picture a tree splitting into two identical trees.

**Get This . . .**

The term *cell* was coined by Robert Hooke, who discovered the cell walls in cork tissue. The boxlike shape cells of cork reminded him of the cells of a monastery. **99**

#1.

The cell is the basic unit of structure and organization in all living things.

#2.

The cell is at the same time both independent and a part of the organism—no matter how large or small the organism.

#3.

All cells come from cells that already exist. A cell divides to form two identical cells.

Blood Donors/Receivers

▶ **Oh** sure, I'll **give** you my blood.
All Blood is what I'll **take**.

There are four blood types in humans: A, B, AB, and O.

A person who has type **AB** blood is able to receive blood from any other type. That person is called a **"Universal Receiver."**

A person who has type **O** blood is able to serve as a donor to a person of any other blood type. That person is called a **"Universal Donor."**

When you remember "Oh sure, I'll give you my blood," think type O can give blood to anyone. When you remember "All Blood is what I'll take," think type AB can take blood from anyone. It may save your life someday.

Imagine the mnemonic to be two lines of a song. Sing the song to your own beat. Especially put emphasis on "Oh sure" and "All Blood," as well as "give" and "take."

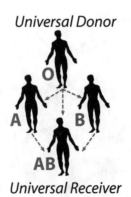

Universal Donor

Universal Receiver

Homeostasis

There is no place like homeostasis!

Homeostasis is the biological process to maintain stability—in other words, to not change. For example, your body reacts to changes in its environment by reacting to restore balance.

If the weather is hot, you may perspire in an attempt to cool down. If the weather is cold, you may shiver or tremble in an attempt to create bodily heat. This is homeostasis.

In the classic film *The Wizard of Oz*, Dorothy clicks her heels and repeats, "There's no place like home." She says this in an attempt to restore her life to the way it was. The change she experiences is dangerous and unhealthy. Going home brings her back to the safety and stability that she needs. This is the crux of homeostasis.

 Repeat the mnemonic out loud as you click your heels!

IT'S YOUR TURN

Think about things you do to maintain stability. And the next time you act on one of those processes—drinking water when you're thirsty, for example—say to yourself, "There's no place like homeostasis, there's no place like homeostasis." Consider what would happened if you didn't follow the process of homeostasis at the time.

Organs of the Digestive System

► The digestive system starts out **MESSI!**

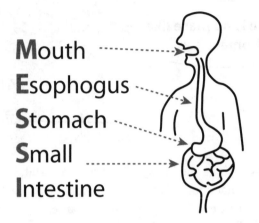

Mouth
Esophogus
Stomach
Small
Intestine

The **digestive system** is composed primarily of the digestive tract, which is basically a long tube that starts at your mouth and ends at your, well, end. There are many contributors to the digestive process, such as saliva from the salivary glands and bile from the gall bladder. But the key organs, starting from the **mouth,** are the **esophagus, stomach, small intestine,** and **large intestine.**

To remember this order of your organs, use the "MESSI" acronym, as shown above. It's an appropriate acronym, because once a beautiful meal enters your mouth, it tends to get messy.

IT'S YOUR TURN

The letters of the digestive system could also be used to create an acrostic. Make up a five word sentence, with words beginning with *M, E, S, S,* and *I.* You can also add *L* and *I* to the end of the acrostic (to make "MESSILI") for large intestine, the last major organ of the digestive tract.

The Five Classes of Vertebrates

B·A·R·F–M!
Birds amphibians reptiles fish mammals

Vertebrates are animals which have a backbone, or a spinal column. Vertebrates have been around a long, long time—more than 500 million years. The vertebrates group includes **birds, amphibians, reptiles, fish** (specifically, bony fish), and **mammals.**

You can remember the five classes of vertebrates with an acronym that includes **"BARF"** and the letter **M.** You could even make that **"M**ike **BARF**ed" and imagine someone named Mike barfing up birds, amphibians, reptiles, fish, and mammals.

Okay, this sounds gross, but here is one way to connect the vertebrates with the mnemonic BARFM. While touching your spine with one hand, pretend to vomit. While you're doing that, make the disgusting sound "Bbbaaaaarrrrrrffffffmmmmmm!"

Lichen

▶ He was a **fun guy**. She was **a gal**. When they met, they took a **likin'** to each other. Now they are living in **Sin-biosis**.

Lichen is a colorful (greens, grays, oranges, or yellows) partnership of a **fungus** and **algae** living together. This type of living arrangement shared between two different species is called **symbiosis.**

To remember this basic fact of lichen, remember the story of the fun guy (sounds like *fungi*) and a gal (sounds like *algae*). What happens when they meet?

Ask a good friend, "What happened when the fun guy met a gal?" The answer is, of course, that they "took a lichen" to each other. Your friend will not understand what you are talking about. But you will always remember what lichen is composed of. (Make sure you try this out with a *very good* friend, because other people might not take a likin' to the lichen story.)

The Speed of Light (Metric)

The **speed of light** is the universe's natural speed limit. It is the fastest speed that anything can travel (that we know), and so it is used to measure distances across the universe. Going at the speed of light, it would take about 4.3 years to reach our closest star, Alpha Centauri. Knowing the speed of light is vital to calculating the distances of faraway objects.

▶ My ingenious astronomy student remembers an easy light mnemonic!

In 1983, the speed of light was set at exactly 299,792,458 meters per second. To remember this precise nine-digit figure, you can use the mnemonic above—where the number of letters in each word represents the digit in the speed.

The Speed of Light (U.S. Units)

▶ Did he eat a light meal?
Nope, this one ate six things a thousand times!

Many people choose to round the speed of light. Using the metric system, you can round to 300 million meters per second. If you choose to use U.S. Customary units, you can use 186,000 miles per second. To remember this, you can imagine that someone ate six things a thousand times (or 186,000 times).

Imagine someone gobbling up a plate of food with six items over and over again at "lightning" speed. This will help you visualize the number—and that the number is about light.

The Order of the Planets

This acrostic helps you remember the order of the planets. The first letter in each word of the sentence is the first letter in the name of a planet. The *M* in "My" stands for Mercury, the *V* in "Very" stands for Venus, and so on. The closest planet to the Sun is Mercury. So, the order of the planets is **Mercury, Venus, Earth, Mars, Jupiter, Saturn, Uranus, Neptune,** and **Pluto.**

The acrostic mentions nine pizzas, so that helps to remind you that there are nine planets! You can also change the acrostic to include other bodies in our solar system, such as the asteroid belt (between Earth and Mars) or the unnamed tenth planet, which astronomers discovered in 2005. (They've given the new planet the temporary nickname "Xena," which would make the acrostic very annoying to revise!)

" *Get This . . .*

Pluto is such a strange planet that its orbit actually crosses Neptune's orbit. That means for 20 years in its 248-year orbit, it is actually closer to the Sun than Neptune. Between 1979 and 1999, students of astronomy had to concoct new mnemonics to remember the order of the planets (with P and N being the last two letters). If you're using this book from 2227 to 2247, you'll have to change the mnemonic as well. **"**

Stellar Classification

▶ **O**nly
Brilliant
Astronomers
Find
Gratification
Knowing
Mnemonics.

Although there are many different types of stars, there are seven that comprise the most common classifications. They are organized by their temperature, from hottest to coolest, in the classes O, B, A, F, G, K, and M.

Stars that are class **O** are extremely hot, very bright, and blue in color.

Stars that are class **B** are very hot, very bright, and blueish-white in color.

Stars that are class **A** stars are hot and whitish-blue in color.

Stars that are class **F** stars are of average temperature and whitish-yellow in color.

Stars that are class **G** stars are slightly cooler and yellow in color. Our Sun is a class G star.

Stars that are class **K** are cooler still and orange in color.

Stars that are class **M** are relatively cold (as far as stars go) and red in color. Class M stars are the most common types of stars in the universe.

The acrostic above reminds you of the order of the star classifications, from hottest to coolest. Notice, if you will, that the color of the stars goes down the color spectrum as each one cools. (Flip to the next two-page spread for the color spectrum!)

Four Spheres of Earth

There are four "geo-spheres" of Earth that interact and shape Earth as we know it. They are the lithosphere, atmosphere, hydrosphere, and biosphere. The four geo-spheres are interconnected and cover all the parts of Earth where humans have interacted (as opposed to the mantle and core of the planet). The names originated from the Greek words for stone, air, water, and life (*litho*, *atom*, *hydro*, and *bio*).

The **lithosphere** is the thin, but solid, shell of planet Earth. It includes the crust and the very top part of the mantle.

The **atmosphere** is the layer of gases surrounding the planet Earth.

The **hydrosphere** is the layer of water that covers the planet Earth, from the water in the clouds to the water at the bottom of the deepest sea.

The **biosphere** is the strip of Earth where life takes place. That includes in air, on land, and under water.

► I wrote the following terms on index cards:

lithosphere, atmosphere, hydrosphere, and biosphere

I walked around my house and placed the cards in the following places:

The lithosphere card is placed on the ground.

The atmosphere card is attached to a string and is hanging from the ceiling.

The hydrosphere card is on the sink.

The biosphere is tied to the leaves of a houseplant.

I walk from one card to the next and follow the path of where the cards are placed to recall information about each sphere.

Move around the room where you have placed the four cards. Put your hand on the ground, jump into the air, turn the water on at the sink, and feel the leaves of the plant.

Electromagnetic Spectrum

The **electromagnetic spectrum** is made up of different kinds of energies. These energies travel in waves of different lengths. The longest waves are radio energies, and the shortest waves are gamma rays. The entire list of energies is radio, microwaves, infrared, visible light, ultraviolet, X-rays, and gamma rays.

There's only one type of energy that we can see with our naked eye—visible light, of course. But that doesn't mean you can ignore the other wavelengths. To remember them, create a set of cards labeled with the different types of waves and place them around your home. See the possible steps below.

▶ Place the radio wave card near a radio.
Place the microwave card near the microwave oven.
Place the infrared card near something red, such as a red apple.
Place the visible light card near a picture of an eye.
Place the ultraviolet card near a picture of something purple or violet.
Place an "X" on a card for X-rays and place the card near a bone if possible.
Place the gamma ray card near a photo of a Gramma.

To remember the order of the wavelengths on the spectrum, walk from the radio wave card to the gamma wave card, in order. As you walk through your home, realize that you are essentially walking down the electromagnetic spectrum, and each card represents the next wavelength by frequency.

IT'S YOUR TURN

What places around your home would be good locations so your can remember the seven different kinds of energy? Choose alternate locations if they have more meaning for you.

The Electromagnetic Spectrum

Radio

Microwaves

Infrared

Visible

Ultraviolet

X-rays

Gamma

The Visible Light Spectrum

▶ Roy G. Biv

Visible light is the part of the electromagnetic spectrum that we can see with our own eyes, yet it's only a very small fraction of the entire electromagnetic spectrum. (Flip to the previous page to see just how many other types of lights there are.)

There are seven basic colors that make up the visible light spectrum. In order from highest frequency to lowest frequency, those colors are **red, orange, yellow, green, blue, indigo,** and **violet.**

You might recognize these colors as the colors in a rainbow. Together, these seven colors form the complete range of colors in the visible light spectrum. The order is scientifically important.

. . . .
IT'S YOUR TURN

Write an acrostic using the seven first letters of the seven colors that form visible light. Can you create a memorable seven-sentence acrostic that will remind you what you're remembering?

Mole Value/Avogadro's Number

You may know a mole as a furry little animal, but it is also one of the most commonly used basic units in chemistry. A **mole** measures the amount of a substance. It is the number of particles in 12 grams of carbon-12. Another way to consider this is that a mole is the amount of a substance where the number of the substance's atomic weight is the same number of grams of the substance.

This amount is known as Avogadro's number. It is approximately **6.02 $\times$ 10^{23}**. (It's closer to 6.0221415 $\times$ 10^{23}, but you won't really need to know that.)

For example, carbon-12 has an atomic weight of 12. So, about 6.02 × 10^{23} atoms of carbon-12 will equal 12 grams. That's one mole of carbon-12.

▶ To help remember this important scientific number, go to your calendar. Open up to October 23. On it, write "MOLE at 6:02." Once you write that, you will know that "MOLE" appears at 6:02, October 23. Those are the numbers in Avogadro's number, 6.02 × 10^{23}.

Perhaps on October 23 (at exactly 6:02), you should feed a mole. Or at least go to the zoo to see one.

"Get This . . .

From 6:02 a.m. to 6:02 p.m. on October 23, chemists and chemistry students celebrate "Mole Day." See www.moleday.org to read about the unofficial holiday. **""**

Chemical Changes vs. Physical Changes

A **chemical change** is a change in which one or more new substances are formed. Burning wood creates a chemical change because new substances, such as carbon dioxide, are formed. A chemical change is irreversible. You cannot un-burn wood or un-fry an egg.

A **physical change** is a change in which no new substances are formed. Ice turning to liquid water, and then into steam, is a physical change. A physical change is reversible. You can re-freeze water to form ice.

Look at the drawings of the two scientists at right. One of them is drinking from a bubbling flask. The bubbling chemicals represent a chemical change, and the scientist turns into a completely new person. He cannot go back to being his old self. This is a chemical change.

The second scientist is drinking from a glass of water with ice. The water and ice represent a physical change (ice melting). After the scientist drinks the water, she is smiling. But she is still the same person. She has not undergone a chemical change.

. . . .
It's Your Turn

Think of as many chemical changes as you can, such as iron rusting. Write each one on a piece of paper with a drawing of the scientist turning into a new person. Then, do the same thing for physical change, with the unchanging scientist by each physical change. If you can, try to make a physical and chemical change on your own. (Ask your parents for permission beforehand because chemical and physical changes can be dangerous!)

Chemical Change

This scientist changes into a new person!
He can't turn back, so this is a chemical change.

Physical Change

This scientist does not undergo an irreversible change.
That means this is a physical change.

Atomic Number of Oxygen

▶ "Octa-gen"

Let's take a trip down memory lane and review some basic chemistry. You may know that elements are made up of atoms and that atoms contain particles called protons, neutrons, and electrons. We identify an element on the periodic table by how many protons it has. This value is known as the **atomic number** of an element. Because an atom has the same number of protons and electrons, the atomic number also tells us the number of electrons.

The element oxygen (O) has an atomic number of 8. That means an atom of oxygen has 8 protons and 8 electrons. Knowing the number of electrons is important because it helps us understand why oxygen forms chemical bonds with certain other elements.

The prefix *octa*– means eight. Think of an octagon, which has 8 sides, or an octopus, which has 8 tentacles. Use the keyword *octa-gen* to help you remember that the atomic number of oxygen is 8.

Draw an octopus named O. At the end of each of its 8 arms, label the word *proton*. (Remember, it's the number of protons that determines the atomic number of an element.)

IT'S YOUR TURN

Take out a sheet of paper. Now, try to list everything you ate for breakfast, lunch, and dinner for the past five days. It's more difficult than you thought it would be, isn't it?

Let's try something else. See if you can describe every outfit you've worn for the past five days. In the process of listing your outfits, did you remember anything else about what you had eaten? Sometimes remembering one specific thing can trigger another associated memory. Especially if you dripped ketchup on your favorite white T-shirt on Tuesday!

The First Two Periods of the Periodic Table

▶ Hungry Heidi Likes Beans But Can Not Often Find N-E

1p   2p   3p   4p   5p 6p 7p   8p   9p 10p

The Periodic Table includes the labels for every element in the known universe. Becoming familiar with its organization can help you to do well in chemistry.

The Periodic Table groups the known elements by their number of protons. Hydrogen has only one proton, so it is the first element in the table. Helium has two protons, so it is it he second element. Lithium has three protons, so it is the third element. Each horizontal row of the periodic table is called a **period.** The first two periods are made up of the elements hydrogen (H), helium (He), lithium (Li), beryllium (Be), boron (B), carbon (C), nitrogen (N), oxygen (O), fluorine (F), neon (Ne).

It helps to know the order of the elements, because then you can always know the number of protons in a particular element. (Quick! If oxygen is the eighth element in the table, then how many protons must it have? Of course, eight!) You can create an acrostic using the letters in the elements to set the order in your mind. For example, if the mnemonic on this page is memorable, you can remember that carbon has six protons—because **C**arbon is represented by the first letter of the word **C**an, which is the sixth word in the acrostic. You just have to recall that "N-E" (online slang for "any") stands for Ne, or neon.

As always, feel free to come up with something different that may have more meaning to you. It can help if the first two letters of the word represent any two-letter element symbols, such as He, Li, or Be. (Notice that the mnemonic above uses words with those first two letters.)

 Sing the mnemonic like a two-verse song. Clap your hands and dance around as you think about Heidi's meal!

Combined Gas Law

▶ Pole Vaulter **1** went **over** the Tower, just like Pole Vaulter **2**.

The **combined gas law** is a combination of three other chemical laws (including Boyle's Law, found on page 221). The combined gas law states that a gas's volume multiplied by its pressure is constant with its temperature. That means you can find the value of the pressure, temperature, or volume using the following formula.

$$\frac{PV}{T} = k$$

In the formula, P is the pressure, V is the volume, T is the temperature, and k is a constant. (Remember that the temperature must be measured in Kelvin.) You can also make comparisons using the combined gas law; you simply set two substances equal to each other using the following formula.

$$\frac{P_1 V_1}{T_1} = \frac{P_2 V_2}{T_2}$$

To remember this complicated formula, use the visual mnemonic on the following page. What's going on? There are two pole vaulters, each flying over a tower. That represents PV over T, or $\frac{PV}{T}$. The two pole vaulters are both doing the same thing, so you could say they are equal. In other words, $\frac{\text{Pole Vaulter}_1}{\text{Tower}_1} = \frac{\text{Pole Vaulter}_2}{\text{Tower}_2}$.

Close your eyes and visualize the two pole vaulters flying through the air. Attaching an action to the mnemonic makes it more memorable. If a tower isn't sticking in your mind, pick another object that starts with the letter T. And if you can find a way to associate the visual mnemonic with what you're trying to remember—the combined gas law—you'll be doubly better off.

$$\frac{P_1 V_1}{T_1} = \frac{P_2 V_2}{T_2}$$

Alkali Metals

▶ **L**ittle
Naked
Kangaroos
Rob
Caeser in
France.

The **alkali metals** are the series of elements in Group 1 of the periodic table, not including hydrogen. They are lithium (Li), sodium (Na), potassium (K), rubidium (Rb), cesium (Cs), and francium (Fr).

The alkali metals are all silver-colored and soft. They are all rarely found in elemental form in nature.

To remember the alkali metals in order from the lightest metals to the heaviest, you can create an acrostic with the letters *L, N, K, R, C,* and *F.* But it helps to do even more than that! For example, if you can make the first two words start with *Li* and *Na,* you'll be in much better shape when trying to remember the elements they represent. In the mnemonic above, each word represents one element—specifically, that it has key letters for the element's symbol.

Likewise, any association to the element only strengthens the mnemonic. For example, France is a natural fit for francium. (The element was discovered at the Radium Institute in Paris, and it was named after the discoverer's native country.)

It's great if you can remember the complete acrostic. But what good is it if you can't remember what the words were supposed to stand for? That's why it's doubly good to connect the information you're learning with a visual image. In this case, you could imagine the little naked kangaroos stealing gray metal jewelry off of Caesar. (Or perhaps you know someone named **C**hris?)

Boyle's Law

▶ To boil water, the **temperature is the same.**

Boyle's Law relates to the relationship of gas at constant temperatures. It follows that the pressure (p) of a gas varies indirectly with its volume (v). The formula, devised by physicist Robert Boyle in 1662, is simply $pv = k$, where k is the constant.

In other words, the volume of a gas will change if the pressure on that gas changes. Increase the pressure and the volume decreases. Decrease the pressure and the opposite happens. But you need to remember that this law only applies when the temperature remains the same!

To remember this critical element of Boyle's Law, consider the temperature at which water boils. At sea level (at a constant pressure) water always 212°F (or 100°C). If you boiled two pots of water on a stove, they would both **boil** at the **same temperature!**

Repeat the mnemonic several times. Concentrate on saying the word *boil* exactly the same way each time. Your voice will help remind you how the temperature is assumed to be the same with Boyle's Law.

Diatomic Elements

▶

Oh,
I
Have
Nice
Closets
For
Brooms.

Diatomic elements are the seven elements that form molecules as two atoms (when in their pure element state). Each word represents a diatomic element. In the order represented by the mnemonic, the diatomic elements are oxygen (0), iodine (I), hydrogen (H), nitrogen (N), chlorine (Cl), fluoride (F), and bromine (Br). For example, oxygen in the atmosphere is almost always in the diatomic state, O_2.

To remember these diatomic elements, you can create an acrostic that sets the seven elements' letters in a way that you will remember them. The mnemonic on this page is especially helpful because the first two letters of *closets* and *brooms* represent each element's symbol—Cl and Br.

Find a broom in your home, and bring it to your closet. (If you have a broom closet already, you're one step ahead!) Put your broom in the closet, and say, "Oh, I have nice closets for brooms!" while stressing the letters of the diatomic elements. Then, try listing the diatomic elements— oxygen, iodine, hydrogen, nitrogen, chlorine, fluoride, and bromine.

Breathe in the O_2 deeply in the closet so you can remember what the broom closet mnemonic is reminding you of.

Ionic Bonds

▶ "I own it" bonds

Chemical bonding is the process by which elements combine to form compounds. For example, hydrogen and oxygen combine to form water (H_2O). Atoms combine with other atoms by losing, gaining, or sharing electrons. Most atoms are stable when they have 8 electrons in their outer energy level. Atoms combine with certain other atoms because they "seek" to become stable.

Table salt is formed through an ionic bond. Sodium, Na, has 1 electron in its outer shell, and chlorine, Cl, has 7 electrons in its outer shell. So, chlorine has a very strong attraction to pull that 1 electron away from sodium to gain a stable outer energy level of 8 electrons. Once that single electron is removed, sodium has a stable outer level too.

This kind of bond, which involves a *transfer* of electrons from one atom to another, is called an **ionic bond.** You can remember that in ionic bonds, one atom takes electrons from another atom using the key phrase "I own it" bonds. Imagine a selfish chlorine atom snatching an electron from the sodium atom, declaring that it belongs to him. Of course, the sodium atom is willing to part with a measly electron if it means he'll be stable too.

In **covalent bonds,** atoms *share* electrons so that their outer energy levels are stable. You can remember that covalent bonds involve sharing because of the prefix *co–*, which means "together with."

Remember that chlorine has 7 electrons in its outer level, so it only needs 1 more electron to be stable. Draw a picture of two chlorine atoms shaking hands, each politely sharing one electron with the other. The pair of chlorine atoms is forming a friendly covalent bond.

Redox Process

▶ **LEO** the Lion goes **GER**!
Lose **E**lectrons = **O**xidation
Gain **E**lectrons = **R**eduction

Reduction and **oxidation** are two fundamental chemical processes whereby electrons are gained and lost. They always occur together, and the process is called **redox** (literally taken from the words *red*uction and *ox*idation).

Oxidation is the process whereby a molecule, atom, or ion loses an electron. This process is accompanied by an increase in oxidation number.

Reduction is the process whereby a molecule, atom, or ion gains an electron. This process is accompanied by a decrease in oxidation number.

Oxidation numbers tell where the electrons are in a reaction. The oxidation number is often referred to as the "charge" on the atom or compound.

To avoid confusing the opposite reactions of oxidation and reduction, you can use the popular mnemonic above with LEO the Lion. Note that the word *Lion* includes an *ion*, which can be part of the oxidation or reduction process.

Example:

$H_2 + F_2 \rightarrow 2HF$ is an example of a redox reaction. The oxidation reaction is $H_2 \rightarrow 2H^+ + 2e^-$ and the reduction reaction is $F_2 + 2e^- \rightarrow 2F^-$. In the oxidation reaction, hydrogen gains an oxidation number of +1. In the reduction reaction, fluorine's oxidation number goes down to −1. The electrons then cancel for the redox reaction:

$$H_2 \rightarrow 2H^+ + 2e^-$$
$$\underline{+ \ 2e^- + F_2 \rightarrow 2F^-}$$
$$H_2 + F_2 \rightarrow 2H^+ + 2F^-$$

Because the ions in $2H^+ + 2F^-$ cancel each other out, $2H^+ + 2F^-$ is equal to 2HF.

· · · · · · · · · · · · ·
IT'S YOUR TURN

LEO the Lion is a common mnemonic to remember the vocabulary of these important chemistry terms. But that doesn't mean it's the best. Come up with your own to help you remember that oxidation is characterized by the loss of electrons, and reduction is characterized by the uptake of electrons.

Formula for Density

▶ In **Den City**, the **M**ountains are over the **V**alley.

To determine how tightly some substances are packed, scientists determined a formula for density as it changes based on a proportion of mass to volume: density = $\dfrac{mass}{volume}$. If more mass is added to the same volume, density increases. If mass is taken away from the same volume, density decreases.

To remember this simple, but essential, formula, consider the fictional town "Den City." In this lovely little town there is a pretty valley and giant mountains. And as you'd expect, the mountains are above the valley. If you can remember $\dfrac{mountains}{valley}$ for "Den City," you can use the first letters to remember $\dfrac{mass}{volume}$.

Example:

Let's say you know that the mass of a substance is 6.4 grams and its volume is 2.5 cm^3. To find the density of the substance, simply set up the equation density = $\dfrac{mass}{volume}$. Substituting the known values, you get density = $\dfrac{6.4\ grams}{2.5\ cm^3}$. That means the density of the substance is 2.56 g/cm^3.

👁 Think about a place you've been that has mountains and a valley. Which is on the top? You may even want to draw your own picture of a mountain over a valley.

PHYSICS

Formula for Speed

▶ The **speed** of the **dragon over** the **tower** is quick!

Speed = Dragon / Tower

Speed is determined by using two measurements: distance and time. The proportion is set such that speed $= \dfrac{\text{distance}}{\text{time}}$. It makes sense too. If it takes you more time to go the same distance, your speed is increasing. If it takes you more time, your speed is decreasing.

Take a look at the drawing above. There is a dragon flying quickly over a tower. It is a visual keyword mnemonic to help you remember how to determine the rate of speed. How? The D in dragon represents the D in distance, and the T in tower represents the T in time. Every time you try to calculate the rate of speed, whether it's a drive to grandma's or a run around the track, you can remember this handy mnemonic.

Example:

If you walk 420 meters in 6 minutes, your speed can be determined with the equation $\dfrac{\text{distance}}{\text{time}}$. Substituting the known values, you get density $= \dfrac{420 \text{ meters}}{6 \text{ minutes}}$, or 70 meters per minute.

IT'S YOUR TURN ICON

A dragon flying over a tower is only one of countless other visual ways to remember the rate of speed. Think of your own "D" and "T" objects, where the "D" is flying over the "T." (Make sure that the "D" object has some speed to it, because that will give you the association to the formula!) Perhaps you've seen a *dove* fly over *Toronto*....

Four Basic Forces

Go
West,
Strong
Earthling.

There are **four basic forces** in nature. Put together, they affect all the matter in the known universe.

Gravitational forces affect any object with mass, such as planets, moons, and suns—as well as you everyone and everything you know. Though the weakest of the four forces, gravity affects matter at the greatest distances.

Weak nuclear forces exist between all pairs of particles. Radioactive decay is a type of weak nuclear force.

Strong nuclear forces act within an atom, maintaining that the elements within its nucleus remain stable. The strong nuclear force is only effective at very short distances.

Electromagnetic forces act between electrical charges. They act on charges, whether alike or opposite.

Recall the four forces by creating an acrostic using the letters *G, W, S,* and *E*—such as "Go West, Strong Earthling!"

. . . .
It's Your Turn

Because the order of the forces is not important, try to rearrange the four letters of the mnemonic to create your own acronym. Use any order you like. Maybe you can rearrange the letters to make the mnemonic more meaningful and memorable to you.

Simple Machines

I Was Pulling Lee's Super Wedgie.

This acrostic tells you the six simple machines that can be used to change the direction or size of a force. These six simple machines are the inclined plane, wheel and axle, pulley, lever, screw, and wedge. The first letter in each word of the sentence is the first letter in the name of the simple machine.

The **i** of "I" stands for the **inclined plane.** An inclined plane is a flat surface like a smooth board set at an angle. When the plane is inclined, or slanted, it can help you move objects. A common inclined plane is a ramp.

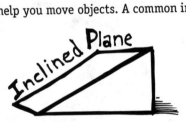

The **w** in "was" stands for the **wheel and axle.** The rotation of the wheel turns the axle, a cylinder-shaped post, causing movement.

The **p** in "pulling" stands for the **pulley,** a cord that wraps around a wheel. As the wheel rotates, the cord moves. Attach a hook to the cord, and you can use the pulley's rotation to raise and lower objects. The word *pulling* is similar to the word *pulley* too!

The **l** in "Lee's" stands for the **lever.** Examples of levers are seesaws, baseball bats, wrenches, and other items that are bars that pivot around a certain point. Think of the claw end of a hammer that you use to pry nails loose.

The **s** in "super" stands for **screw,** which is an inclined plane wrapped around a cylinder. For example, you could turn a metal screw through wood—and each turn would help you move the metal through the wood.

The **w** in "wedgie" stands for **wedge,** which can be used to push things apart or split them. An axe blade is a wedge. Think of the edge of the blade as two smooth slanted surfaces meeting at a point. The word *wedgie* is similar to the word *wedge* too!

Think of someone you know whose name begins with "L"—Larry, Lisa, Lee, Lana, anyone. Review the mnemonic again with your friend's name. Then, imagine you were pulling their Super Wedgie! (Don't actually do it, though, because it's mean and wedgies are painful!) Review the mnemonic again and visualize each simple tool with the first letter of each word.

Properties of Waves

Waves have different properties. The highlighted words in the mnemonic are different properties of waves. As you read, you should visualize yourself physically walking through the surroundings that are described, and experiencing the events in the order in which they occur.

▶ I have written the words *frequency, amplitude, wavelength, crest,* and *trough* on index cards. I walk around my home and put the cards in places where they can help me remember the information.

First, I place the **frequency** card near a calendar. I use the calendar to count the number of days in a week, a month, until my birthday, and so on. Then, I put the **amplitude** card on my bed. My bed is where I take a rest. Next, I put the **wavelength** card near a ruler on my desk. I can use my ruler to measure distance. Next, I tape the **crest** card on my bedroom ceiling. My ceiling is very high. Finally, I place the **trough** card on the floor. The floor is low.

Frequency describes the number of wavelengths occurring in a given unit of time.

The **amplitude** usually describes the height of the crest of a wave when the wave is in the rest position.

The **wavelength** is the distance between successive crests or successive troughs.

The **crest** of a wave is the highest point of a wave. It is the maximum distance upward from the rest position.

The **trough** of a wave is the lowest point of a wave. It is the maximum distance downward from the rest position.

The Properties of Waves

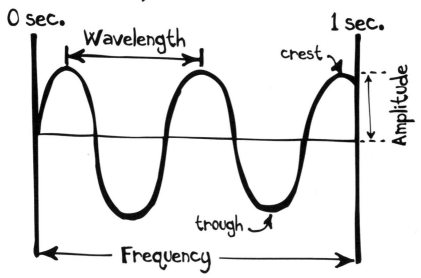

Walk around your house and find the five cards about waves. Touch the numbers on the calendar when you find the frequency card. Put your head on the pillow when you find the amplitude card. Measure a distance with the ruler when you find the wavelength card. Reach up to the ceiling when you find the crest card. Touch the floor when you find the trough card.

The Components of an Atom

An atom contains three types of particles: **protons, neutrons,** and **electrons.** Protons are positively charged, and electrons are negatively charged. Neutrons have no charge. Look to the words for clues to remind you of that. Specifically, notice that the words *proton* and *neutron* start with the same letters as the designation of their charge.

▶ Proton = Positive
Neutron = Neutral

The electron is the only part of an atom that is not contained within its nucleus. (The nucleus is surrounded by a cloud of negative electrons.)

▶ To remember the location and polarity of the electron, imagine an image of the sun as a representation of an atom's nucleus. The heat lines coming off of it represent minus signs (negative). Those are the electrons. This simple image of the sun will help you to remember that negative particles surround the center of the atom.

Draw a giant circle that represents an atom. Then draw a plus sign and the number 0 inside the circle you drew. Be sure to draw minus signs as lines on the outside of the circle. The negative part of the atom goes on the outside too.

Energy Levels of Electrons (Electron Shells)

▶ **S**ome **P**eople **D**on't **F**loss.

The letters ***s, p, d***, and ***f*** designate the electron configurations of atoms. Each letter represents an orbit that an electron may travel in around the atom, with the *s* orbit being closest to the nucleus.

s subshells carry up to 2 electrons and have 1 orbital.

p subshells carry up to 6 electrons and have 3 orbitals.

d subshells carry up to 10 electrons and have 5 orbitals.

f subshells carry up to 14 electrons and have 7 orbitals.

These seemingly random letters originally stood for sharp, principal, diffuse, and fundamental. But those descriptions were long ago deemed inaccurate. Because there can be more than four orbital levels, scientists use additional lettering beyond *F*. Fortunately for us, the lettering is alphabetical following the fourth level. So the first 11 orbits, for example, are labeled *s, p, d, f, g, h, i, k, l, m,* and *n*. (No, we didn't forget *j*—it's not used in the orbital levels of atoms.)

To remember the order of the first four energy levels, create an acrostic using the letters *s, p, d,* and *f* (in that order, of course). Some People Don't Floss is one such acrostic.

IT'S YOUR TURN

Maybe everyone you know *does* floss. (Good for them! Flossing is very good for your teeth and gums!) So try to think of other verbs that you could substitute for *floss* in the acrostic.

Watts

▶ **What** thief could steal a **jewel** every **second**?

The **watt** is the unit we use to measure power. It is named after James Watt, who helped develop the steam engine. You have probably heard of watts in terms of the powers of lightbulbs. Their energy output is most often measured in watts, usually in the range of 50–100 watts.

One watt is equal to **one joule per second.** A joule is a measure of unit of work or energy, based on the force of one newton moving one meter. To remember the value of one watt, consider the chaining mnemonic above.

Say the mnemonic out loud. Emphasize "what," "jewel," and "second" to help you remember how the three are connected. Ask a stranger on the street this very question and measure the energy he or she uses to run away in watts.